HOW TO BUILD A HOUSE OF PRAYER

A Practical Guide to Launching and Leading Prayer Rooms

Brad Stroup

Copyright ©2024 Brad Stroup.

All rights reserved. No part of this book may be used or reproduced in any manner without written permission from the publisher, except in the case of brief quotations in articles and reviews.

ISBN 978-1-951611-60-6

Published by Presence Pioneers Media.

Printed in the United States of America.

Unless otherwise noted, Scripture passages are taken from the Holy Bible, New International Version®, NIV®. Copyright ©1973, 1978, 1984, 2011 by Biblica, Inc.™ Used by permission of Zondervan. All rights reserved worldwide. www.zondervan.com The "NIV" and "New International Version" are trademarks registered in the United States Patent and Trademark Office by Biblica, Inc.™

Passages marked NKJV taken from the New King James Version®. Copyright © 1982 by Thomas Nelson. Used by permission. All rights reserved.

CONTENTS

Preface / 1

Unit 1: Your Part in the Prayer Movement
    Session 1: Let Prayer Arise / 7
    Session 2: Identifying Your Expression / 17
    Session 3: Mandates of a Missions Base / 25

Unit 2: Leadership
    Session 4: The Call to Build God's House / 33
    Session 5: Building Your Team / 39
    Session 6: Things to Embrace and Things to Avoid / 45

Unit 3: Laying a Foundation
    Session 7: Casting & Keeping the Vision / 57
    Session 8: Growth Strategies / 63
    Session 9: A Basic Prayer Model / 71

Unit 4: Development
    Session 10: Taking a Look at TPR's Departments / 83
    Session 11: Financing Your Work / 93

Unit 5: Starting to Build
    Session 12: Administrative Steps / 101
    Session 13: From the Ground Up / 109
    Session 14: Expanding Once You're Established / 115

    About the Author / 127
    Recommended Resources / 129

Preface

My story begins in September of 2005 when my life drastically and suddenly changed forever. In one moment everything I thought I knew about my life and calling shifted. It took years to put the pieces together to see how the Lord was weaving together my past ministry and calling to what would become my permanent future. Really what happened to me September 12, 2005 is the reason that this handbook exists, and it's marked my life in a way that no other experience has.

Before that time I had been serving as a career missionary in the nation of Mali, and I felt strongly that was my calling for life. A time came, however, when I felt the Lord lead me to come off the mission field and return home. For what I did not know and for how long I was unsure. I did so quite reluctantly, and upon return I was restless, all the while busying my mind trying to find a way back out into doing what I considered to be "the real work." i.e. foreign missions.

One day after over a year of this restless waiting, I was sitting on my couch reading a book when the Holy Spirit hijacked my peaceful reading and spoke the clearest statement to me that I had ever heard from Him. It was totally unprovoked and the information was totally foreign to my mind. As I sat reading, the voice of the Lord broke in quite powerfully and said the following statement: "Start a daily prayer meeting tomorrow morning at five a.m. and don't stop until I come back."

My life was over. How could I get back into the mission field if I was locked into daily prayer meetings in Arlington, Texas? How was I going to get up every day at 5am, earlier really, and why was it soo early? I was doomed. I was 100% positive I had just received clear direction from the Lord for the rest of my life. The statement resounded in my being; His presence had me on the floor as the words "start a daily prayer meeting tomorrow morning at five a.m. and don't stop until I come back" repeated again and again. My life was now over and five a.m. prayer meetings would be my lot until… oh yeah until when? Until you "come back?" What in the world did that mean?

When I began this journey, I didn't have anything to contribute to a conversation about the House of Prayer, let alone strategies about how one would go about building such a thing. In fact, when we started holding those daily prayer meetings, none of us were thinking at all about 24/7 prayer or a missions base or full time singers and musicians. I certainly didn't have in mind that our experience would lead me to write a handbook on the subject years later.

Some months into the journey, however, the Lord began to reveal that He had more in store for our little prayer meetings than simply five a.m. It became clear that we were to build a 24/7 prayer furnace and to do what we could to help establish 24/7 prayer across our region and beyond. This began the painful process of finding out that no one knows how to do such a thing. I asked everyone I could, "How do you build the House of Prayer—is there a handbook anywhere?" That question proved futile time and time again. I was given only bad answers and blank looks. Oh, and one more annoying response that I must have heard half a dozen times. "A handbook? No, not that I know of…maybe you're supposed to write it."

This work represents the lessons of years of coming up short, having to reinvent answers, coming up with solutions to problems nobody really understands and figuring out the practical steps of how to establish a house of prayer and then maintaining it with little to no resources. I was surprised at how great of a joy it was to write this handbook; I was motivated by the hope that I could save people many headaches by simply providing ideas that had been proven to work at least once. I pray this will become a helpful resource to many who embark to pioneer houses of prayer in the coming years.

Blessings,
Brad Stroup
Director, *The Prayer Room Missions Base*

UNIT I

Your Part in the Prayer Movement

Session 1: Let Prayer Arise

Session 2: Identifying Your Expression

Session 3: Mandates of a Missions Base

Session One: Let Prayer Arise

I. **Prayer Movement in the 21st Century:**

   A. **History of the Prayer Movement:**
      1. Moses' Tabernacle
      2. David's Tabernacle
      3. Solomon's Temple
      4. Eight Restorations of the Tabernacle Worship (Leaders of Judah)

   B. **What is Happening Globally:**
   Since 1999 there has been a global explosion of the House of Prayer in the Earth. While history saw thousands, we are now seeing millions participating in the Prayer Movement with night and day expressions across the Earth.

   C. **Crescendo of Global Church Unity:**
   The culmination of God's plan is to have a unified Praying Church. In the Prayer Movement you will commonly hear the term thrown around that we are praying for a "change in the expression of Christianity." This isn't at all cultic. The change we are referring to is actually to revert back to the prayer lifestyle of the early Church; traditions that have been mostly lost in modern day. The explosive growth of the Prayer Movement since 1999 is a sign that God has already begun to bring about that shift in Church Culture.

   D. **Your Role in the Drama:**
   The fact that you are here reading a House of Prayer handbook means you have some role in that global crescendo. He is enlisting leaders from all the nations and from every background to accomplish the massive undertaking of calling His Bride into Her place. Not just as co-laborers in works of justice, but also in intercession as Christ Himself always lives to intercede.

> *...but because Jesus lives forever, he has a permanent priesthood. Therefore he is able to save completely those who come to God through him, because he always lives to intercede for them (Hebrews 7:24-25).*

II. Scriptural Basis for Night-and-Day Prayer:

A. Prominence in Scripture:
24-hour worship and intercession is a surprisingly large theme in the scripture (1Ch. 9:33; Le. 6:12-14, 24:2-4; Ps. 134:1, 135:1-3; Is. 62:6-7; Lk. 18:1-8; 1Th. 3:10; 1Ti. 5:5; Re. 5:8, 12:10). The concept of night-and-day prayer is deeply rooted in the scriptures and is revealed in several Biblical principles.

B. God Watches Over Us 24 Hours a Day:
God was the first watchman ever to be posted; He gives watch over His children night and day. The Lord is righteous and so we are to act righteously, and where the Lord operates in perfect wisdom so we are to pursue wisdom. So too we are to emulate God's character in giving watch.

> *My help comes from the LORD, the Maker of heaven and earth...he who watches over you will not slumber; indeed, he who watches over Israel will neither slumber nor sleep. The LORD watches over you...he will watch over your life; the LORD will watch over your coming and going both now and forevermore (Psalm 121:2-8).*

C. Jesus Always Lives to Make Intercession:
Jesus is positioned at the right hand of the Father. He always lives to make intercession for the saints. Jesus prays night and day.

> *Now there have been many of those priests, since death prevented them from continuing in office; but because Jesus lives forever, he has a permanent priesthood. Therefore he is able to save completely those who come to God through him, <u>because he always lives to intercede</u> for them (Hebrews 7:23-25).*

> *Who is he that condemns? <u>Christ Jesus</u>, who died—more than that, who was raised to life—is at the right hand of God and <u>is also interceding for us</u> (Romans 8:34).*

D. God's Preferred Environment:
The eternal God could have chosen any environment He wanted to surround Himself in Heaven. He could have chosen a quiet water brook where He would rest, or He could have chosen a construction site where He would manufacture His created

order. But He didn't; He chose an atmosphere of unceasing prayer and worship to surround His throne. This really tells us a lot about His priorities. Revelation 4-5 makes it clear that the angels, the Four Living Creatures and the 24 elders worship God literally night-and-day. Heaven brings forth worship and intercession 24 hours a day.

> *In the center, around the throne, were four living creatures… <u>Day and night they never stop saying: "Holy, holy, holy is the Lord God Almighty</u>, who was, and is, and is to come." Whenever the living creatures give glory, honor and thanks to him…the twenty-four elders fall down before him who sits on the throne, and worship him…and say: "You are worthy, our Lord and God, to receive glory and honor and power" (Revelation 4:6-11).*

E. On Earth as it is in Heaven:

The Bible teaches us to pray that God's will be done on earth as it is in heaven. God calls us to watch and pray with Him. This is why we believe that praise, worship and intercession should also take place on earth for 24 hours a day. The only way in which this can become reality is by establishing literal 24-hour prayer watches.

> *"Our Father in heaven, hallowed be your name, your kingdom come, your will be done on earth as it is in heaven" (Matthew 6:9-10).*

III. New Testament Foundation of Corporate Prayer:

The concept of night and day prayer is not a new one. Prayer as a lifestyle is not merely a meeting that one attends periodically; it is foundational to Biblical New Testament Christianity. That which we are labeling "The Prayer Movement" is merely a restoration of the lifestyle of the early Church.

A. Jesus' Familiar Exhortations on Prayer:

> *"When you pray…"(Matthew 6:9).*
> *"Watch and pray…"(Matthew 26:41).*
> *"will not God bring…justice for (those)…who cry out to him day and night?" (Luke 18:7).*
> *"Be always on the watch and pray…"(Luke 21:36).*

B. The Apostles' Repeated Exhortations on Prayer:

> *Be joyful in hope, patient in affliction, faithful in prayer (Romans 12:12).*
> *…pray…on all occasions…be alert and always keep on praying… (Ephesians 6:18).*
> *…in everything, by prayer and petition…present your requests to God*

(Philippians 4:6).
Devote yourselves to prayer…(Colossians 4:2).
Pray continually…(1Thessalonians 5:17).
The end of all things is near. Therefore…pray (1Peter 4:7).

C. The Lifestyle of the 1st Century Church:

They all joined together constantly in prayer… (Acts 1:14).
They devoted themselves to…prayer (Acts 2:42).
"We will…give our attention to prayer…" (Acts 6:3-4).

IV. The Priesthood of the Old Testament:

A. The Fire on the Altar Must be Kept Burning:

"The fire on the altar must be kept burning; it must not go out. Every morning the priest is to add firewood and arrange the burnt offering on the fire and burn the fat of the fellowship offerings on it. The fire must be kept burning on the altar continuously; it must not go out" (Leviticus 6:12-13).

B. The Two Most Important Priestly Tasks:

1. To make intercession:
This was accomplished through the prayers of the priests and the offerings sacrificed on behalf of the community (Leviticus 14:31).
2. To offer praise and worship:
The fire on the altar was a symbol of the continued praise, worship, intercession and reconciliation done by the priests (Exodus 24:1).

V. New Testament Priesthood:

A. Jesus High Priest of the New Testament Priesthood:

The Old Testament priesthood was incomplete; but instead of being done away with, it was replaced with another priesthood. To have done away with it would have made sacrifices unnecessary; to replace it would mean a redefining of those sacrifices.

If perfection could have been attained through the Levitical priesthood (for on the basis of it the law was given to the people), why was there still need for another priest to come—one in the order of Melchizedek, not in the order of Aaron? For when there is a change of the priesthood, there must also be a change of the law (Hebrews 7:11-12).

Session One: Let Prayer Arise

B. Defining the New Sacrificial System:

As New Testament believers, we have been called priests. Priests must offer sacrifices night and day (Le. 6:12). The sacrifices of the New Testament Priesthood, however, are prayer and praise not animals and grain.

> *...you also, like living stones, are being built into a spiritual house to <u>be a holy priesthood</u>, <u>offering spiritual sacrifices acceptable</u> to God through Jesus Christ (1Peter 2:5).*

> *But you are a chosen people, a <u>royal priesthood</u>, a holy nation, a people belonging to God, <u>that you may declare the praises of him</u> who called you out of darkness into his wonderful light (1Peter 2:9).*

C. A Kingdom of Priests:

God designed things in such a manner that as followers of God we are of a new order, a priestly order. We are called a kingdom of priests. This means that whether or not we operate in the function of priest (based off of whether we use our time praying), we are positionally called priests before God. It makes more sense to go ahead and embrace this unchangeable identity.

> *"Now if you obey me fully and keep my covenant, then out of all nations you will be my treasured possession. <u>Although the whole earth is mine, you will be for me a kingdom of priests</u> and a holy nation" (Exodus 19:5-6).*

> *"...and has made us to be a kingdom and priests to serve his God and Father—to him be glory and power for ever and ever! Amen" (Revelation 1:6).*

> *"You have made them to be a kingdom and priests to serve our God, and they will reign on the earth" (Revelation 5:10).*

D. Millennial Priesthood:

The priesthood will still be intact in running the administration of the Millennial Kingdom while Christ is on Earth.

> *"Blessed and holy are those who have part in the first resurrection. The second death has no power over them, <u>but they will be priests of God</u> and of Christ and will reign with him for a thousand years" (Revelation 20:6).*

E. We will be Called Priests Forever:

We will be called priests forever; all of us. This is not the case for any other of the so called "callings." Long after evangelism ceases, after mercy deeds are done away with, after there is no one left to heal, the ministry of intercession and the role of the eternal priesthood (He. 5:6, 6:20, 7:3, 17, 21, 24) will remain.

F. God's Government:

God will run His government according to intercession forever. He runs the world now in connection to the prayers of the saints, both those on earth (2Ch. 7:14) and those in Heaven (Re. 6:9-11). Just because this age will end and another begins doesn't mean that God ceases to increase His Kingdom. Nor does He change His eternal administration of government employing the participation of His people through prayer.

> *"Of the increase of his government and peace there will be no end. He will reign on David's throne and over his kingdom, establishing and upholding it with justice and righteousness from that time on and forever. The zeal of the LORD Almighty will accomplish this" (Isaiah 9:7).*

VI. Night and Day Prayer for God's Purposes:

A. God Himself Appoints Watchmen:

Watchmen were placed on the walls of cities to protect its people and to safeguard it (Is. 1:6-8, 62:6; Ez. 22:30). God uses this same term to describe intercessors to make the point of how important their watching is to the safety of a community. He calls intercessors to be posted on the walls and to pray for the fulfillment of all of God's promises, many of which are uniquely tied to the events and specific purposes God has for the End Times.

> *"I have posted watchmen on your walls, O Jerusalem; they will never be silent day or night. You who call on the LORD, give yourselves no rest, and give him no rest till he establishes Jerusalem and makes her the praise of the earth" (Isaiah 62:6-7).*

1. God appointed:
   It is God Himself who appoints the watchmen (intercessors) to pray on behalf of His purposes.
2. The watching must be unbroken:
   Watchmen must corporately stand at their posts before Him 24 hours a day. This was never intended in any context to be the assignment of one individual to stand post 24/7 for days on end; that is impossible because eventually they will fall asleep. The concept is 24/7 watching accomplished through shifts of people in rotation on the wall.
3. The watching must continue until:
   The watchmen may not keep silent or allow Him to rest until all His promises have been fulfilled. God's Word holds thousands of promises for His children and Scripture instructs us to continually pray for the fulfillment of these promises.

Session One: Let Prayer Arise

B. Breakthrough of Justice is Tied to Night & Day Prayer:

In Luke 18 God promises that He will bring justice, that is set the wrong things right; crime, violence, poverty, abortion, drug abuse, corruption, immorality, injustice, broken marriages and the AIDS epidemic. He ties this break-in of justice to us calling out to Him night-and-day.

> *Then Jesus told his disciples a parable to show them that they should always pray and not give up.*
> *"...And will not God bring about justice for his chosen ones, who cry out to him day and night? Will he keep putting them off? I tell you, he will see that they get justice, and quickly. However, when the Son of Man comes, will he find faith on the earth?" (Luke 18:1, 7-8)*

VII. Corporate Benefits of Night & Day Prayer:

A. Become the House of Prayer:

A 24/7 prayer watch will be one way the Church can fulfill God's command to be a house of prayer for the nations (Is. 56:7). By implementing 24/7 prayer watches, the Body is able to take responsibility and stand as watchmen on the walls for the Church worldwide, for their own communities, their country and the nations.

B. The Great Harvest of Souls:

24/7 prayer will bring in the great harvest. We know that God desires that none would perish (2Pe. 3:9), and we know that He leaves much of the outcome up to us in relationship to prayer (Mt. 7:7-8). But He doesn't exactly tell us how much prayer is necessary.

1. Directly told that prayer is connected to the harvest:

    > *Then he said to his disciples, "The harvest is plentiful but the workers are few. Ask the Lord of the harvest, therefore, to send out workers into his harvest field" (Matthew 9:37-38).*

2. If we don't pray:

    We need to understand that with regard to everything, but for our argument the harvest, that if we don't pray there really is a correlation to nothing results that we see happening.

    > *You do not have, because you do not ask God. When you ask, you do not receive, because you ask with wrong motives, that you may spend what you get on your pleasures (James 4:2-3).*

3. How much prayer is required:

There's no direct answer; indirectly, however, if we know that a little prayer yields a little result and much prayer yields a much larger result, then we want to pray as much as is physically possible.

> *"Ask and it will be given to you; seek and you will find; knock and the door will be opened to you. <u>For everyone who asks receives; he who seeks finds; and to him who knocks, the door will be opened</u>" (Matthew 7:7-8).*

C. Seeing the Youth Turn to God:

We are praying for this generation of young people to return to God and to become God-fearing men and women who will carry out the Great Commission and the Great Commandment.

> *The hearts called to the Lord. Then I, Jeremiah, cried, "O wall of the Daughter of Zion, <u>let tears run down like a river night-and-day</u>; give yourself no rest; let not your eyes stop shedding tears. Arise, cry out in the night, at the beginning of the night watches; pour out your heart like water before the face of the Lord. Lift up your hands toward Him <u>for the lives of your young children</u>, who faint from hunger at the head of every street" (Lamentations 2:18-19, NKJV).*

D. Unity in the Church:

The concept of 24/7 prayer ministries promotes unity among believers in a region because we can all focus on the same issues and pray together for them. This binds churches and even members from different denominations closer together in God's purposes for their city and nation. If Jesus had to pray for the Church to be unified, then it is going to take prayer to see it become reality.

> *"My prayer is not for them alone. I pray also for those who will believe in me through their message, that all of them may be one, Father, just as you are in me and I am in you...May they be brought to complete unity to let the world know that you sent me and have loved them even as you have loved me" (John 17:20-23).*

E. Strengthens Corporate Responsibility:

So much of God's exhortations are to the corporate people of God. The concept is that He wants His corporate people to take responsibility for what is wrong, out of place and lacking. Night & day prayer communities help every intercessor and prayer group to understand that we have a corporate responsibility to see God's purposes fulfilled. This strengthens us to know that we are not alone, nor should we act like we are.

F. Empowerment for Impact:

Through prayer we receive power from God (through the Holy Spirit) to be witnesses of the love, salvation and compassion of Jesus and to take it to the ends of the earth. There is no greater expression of prayer on Earth than where corporate, unending prayer and worship is established. History shows that wherever there has been night & day prayer, there has been huge impact made on the communities and world surrounding it.

VIII. Personal Benefits of Night & Day Prayer:

A. Personal Perseverance:

Establishing a night-and-day prayer community helps us all to persevere in prayer. Quite simply, with an infrastructure in place of regular corporate prayer we will all prayer more. We also tend to be able to persevere on issues that would otherwise be neglected.

You need to persevere so that when you have done the will of God, you will receive what he has promised (Hebrews 10:36).

B. Fellowship with God:

Prayer brings us into deeper fellowship with God; it is the basis of a life of intimacy with Jesus. The deeper we fellowship with Jesus, the more He reveals His heart to us. The purpose of prayer is to strengthen us to live the First and Second Greatest Commandments (to love God and to love people). This is a prerequisite to see the fulfillment of the Great Commission.

"Love the Lord your God with all your heart and with all your soul and with all your mind.' This is the first and greatest commandment" (Matthew 22:37-38).

C. Better Disciples of Christ:

A praying saint is far better equipped in love, in service and in obedience. To build upon the foundation of prayer causes us to live as better disciples of Jesus, willing to follow Him wherever He goes.

And pray in the Spirit on all occasions with all kinds of prayers and requests. With this in mind, be alert and always keep on praying for all the saints (Ephesians 6:18).

D. Continual Prayer is God's Will for Us:

Be joyful always; <u>pray continually</u>; give thanks in all circumstances, for this is God's will for you in Christ Jesus (1 Thessalonians 5:16-18).

Session Two: Identifying Your Expression

I. **Understanding What God has Given You:**

   A. **God is Orchestrating Great Diversity of Expression:**
      1. Vastness:
         The Lord's End Time Prayer Movement transcends culture, denominations, gender, language, ethnicity, geography, ideology, social class, and whatever else there may be that has traditionally separated the Church.
      2. Styles of ministry:
         As a result of this diversity, there are many ways that the House of Prayer looks throughout the Earth. And even within ministries that are structured similarly, there are differences in focus.

   B. **Getting God's Blueprints for Your Ministry:**
      1. Saying yes to the call:
         If the Lord has already begun to stir your heart about co-partnering with Him to build His House of Prayer, then congratulations you've begun the most incredible and potentially difficult ministry in existence.
      2. Praying for direction:
         Now it is time to ask God what expression He is calling you to. Many of you may already have some ideas about what He is speaking to you. You will want to begin to write these things down so that you will be able to communicate your plan to those you want to approach about helping you.
      3. Details of what it will look like:
         a. Where will you meet?
         b. When will you meet?
         c. How will the meetings flow?
         d. What focus will you have?

HOW TO BUILD A HOUSE OF PRAYER

C. Defining Principle of the House of Prayer:

1. It is written:

    Jesus reiterates for us what the prophet Isaiah had earlier identified was on the heart of the Lord, stating that the House of God would be called the House of Prayer.

    "...these I will bring to my holy mountain and give them <u>joy in my house of prayer</u>. Their burnt offerings and sacrifices will be accepted on my altar; for <u>my house will be called a house of prayer for all nations</u>" (Isaiah 56:7).

    "It is written," he said to them, "'<u>My house will be called a house of prayer</u>,' but you are making it a 'den of robbers'" (Matthew 21:13).

2. Clearing up the matter:

    Anybody can have a prayer meeting from time to time, but that doesn't make them a House of Prayer, nor does it mean their efforts are invaluable. But a House of Prayer is one that is defined by prayer; it is the primary thing that occurs there, it happens regularly or constantly, but not once or twice a week. Prayer is still valuable no matter how infrequently it occurs, even if it only happens on Easter, but we mustn't confuse what the term House of Prayer means. To be a House of Fill-in-the-Blank means that whatever is in that blank (whether Prayer, Pancakes, Wax, Horrors) is the defining characteristic of that organization or group; and to be truthful, it must be what predominately occurs there.

3. Event vs lifestyle:

    We are talking about the difference between hosting an event and establishing a culture of prayer. It is very easy to gather people together to an event; in our culture it's not even so difficult to gather people together for a weekly service. But prayer has to become a lifestyle in order to maintain a House of Prayer.

4. Determination:

    Any person who feels called to it can start a daily prayer meeting (even M-F), especially if there is a team of people who are rallied together. It takes serious determination to fight through the smallness, but it isn't out of the range of anyone to start and hold down prayer meetings on a regular basis. This is the very heartbeat required for a House of Prayer to exist. Liking prayer isn't enough; it takes leadership setting their face like flint to ensure that prayer continues to happen.

D. Major Expressions:

In the following sections we will be taking a look at each of the major expressions of the House of Prayer. This isn't meant to be an exhaustive list, merely an identification of what is out there. There are 2 major categories with offshoots and hybrids of each; local church expressions and para-church expressions. Looking at these structures may be very helpful for you as you are trying to identify where you fit.

II. Local Church Vs Para-Church:
A. Strengths of Local Church Expressions:
1. Finances:
   Finances are often more easily accessible than if you were trying to do something on your own. Even a hundred dollar a month budget will really help get things started at first.
2. Facilities:
   Facilities are often more easily accessible than if you had to find them on your own. Typically if the leadership of your church is willing to begin a focus on prayer, they will also be able to provide some meeting space, maybe even a small room that can be set aside just for this purpose.
3. Influence:
   You immediately have access to a group of intercessors from your local church as well as the opportunity to call the entire congregation to come be a part at whatever level they are able.
4. Unified vision:
   You provide a way for your church to unify around a common vision and to build strong relationships in prayer.

B. Difficulties of Local Church Expressions:
1. Limited external participation:
   As a local church it will be difficult to get people from other congregations to commit to be with you in your prayer times.
2. Limited human resources:
   You will be capped for human resources (i.e. intercessors), having to rely solely on your congregation for worship leaders and intercessors. Historically it has been very difficult to build additional prayer meetings after you have gotten the initial surge and have things fairly well established.
3. At the mercy of the head pastor:
   There are many surprising bumps and hurdles along the way with regard to the leadership's view and agenda for congregation-based HOPs. If the head pastor is not actively involved in the vision and the prayer meetings themselves, this route may be difficult.

C. Strengths of Para-Church Expressions:
1. Size:
   There is no limit to how many groups you can appeal to to get involved, so the size of your House of Prayer isn't limited.
2. Leader run:
   No one pastor can shut down your operation, which is always a potential case with a congregation-based HOP. Keeping the head pastor on board with the vision is very important in those instances.
3. Unifying in their city:
   These ministries can be extremely unifying works for the Church in a region.
4. Long term financial advantage:
   Once the initial financial hurdles have been overcome, you actually have an advantage. Until then you face a very difficult aspect of the para-church expression; it may take years to get to a point of stability. But once you do, for the rest of your years your ministry has no cap to how much money you can raise.
5. Percentage of budget:
   In all of the local church expressions, only a percentage of the budget will be allocated to the House of Prayer; but in the para-church environment, 100% of the resources are available for its expansion.

D. Difficulties of Para-Church Expressions:
1. Lack of leadership support:
   As a para-church organization, it is often difficult to get local pastors to come together to help build prayer which means you start off very small, typically just a small group of friends and family.
2. Lack of finances:
   Finances are often difficult to acquire. It can require a lot of time in order to build up a sufficient operating budget.
3. Lack of influence:
   You often start off with very few intercessors and because it's not the prayer ministry of a local church, you have almost no way to cast the vision to a large group. You have to be very strategic in order to acquire opportunities and gain more intercessors.

III. Expressions of the Praying Church:

A. Prayer Groups:

Session 2: Identifying Your Expression

The defining characteristic of a prayer group is that it is more informal in nature. There probably is not a vision for it to grow into a large corporate prayer gathering. Its fruit and function is in its simplicity; it can happen anywhere with as few as two people. Such initiatives are beginning to take root as a staple expression of the Prayer Movement. These meetings vary in meeting location, ranging from living rooms and finished out garages to back yard barns and break rooms. These groups are committed to daily prayer meetings (or at least 5 days a week) and may or may not have aspirations to increase that number of prayer meetings.
1. Family prayer times
2. In the workplace
3. Friends in dorms or wherever

B. Prayer Ministries:
These are organized groups that carry a specific calling and vision. The leadership of these various prayer ministries is working toward a particular mandate that increases the level of prayer in their sphere of influence in a particular way. They are not trying to build 24/7 prayer, but rather their efforts are aimed at some aspect of launching, stirring or training so that others would pray more.

C. Local Church with a Prayer Focus:
In this expression, a local church decides to devote a measure of energy to hosting, and probably training on prayer (it can look many different ways). Those in this expression type may utilize the web stream of an established house of prayer or corporate sets with or without worship leaders.
1. Prayer department at the church: hundreds of examples
2. Aspect of small group life: Home groups that include prayer
3. Prayer slots: Many local congregations
4. Boiler rooms: 24/7 Prayer (Pete Greig)

D. A Praying Church:
The major difference between this expression and a Local Church with a Prayer Focus is the level of commitment from the leadership and the church as a whole. A Praying Church is where the head leadership of the church commits to daily set times of prayer (or 5 days a week). The pastor actually requires his staff to attend these meetings as part of what they do as staff. Involvement of the rest of the congregation is encouraged and regularly pushed from the pulpit.
1. Pastor involved: Grace Community

2. Pastor driven: Corey Jones at Crossroads Tabernacle

E. **Campus Ministry:**
   This speaks of any version of a prayer ministry that meets as little as 5 times per week (Monday-Friday) actually on the campus of a college or university. Their long-term goals may vary, but maintaining prayer from semester to semester stays as priority. These groups either focus on times of corporate prayer or by operating a shared prayer closet.
   1. Centralized multi-org: CHOP Austin
   2. Campus department: CFNI
   3. Prayer closet concept: UTA BSM
      This is where a ministry focuses on having one person at a time in their prayer room (it can be even as small as a closet). With prayer closets, it is intended that the majority of the time the HOP operates is through hour long single man shifts. Typically the intercessors are given prayer guides or direction in some form to know what to focus their prayers on, as well as providing a strategy for how to spend the committed time.

F. **City Wide Prayer Center:**
   This expression is a city-wide work that encompasses the various styles, models and callings of the local congregations in that area. It forms when different churches each take responsibility for 1 or more watches per week. They implement their own model of prayer and, to some degree, their own vision for why they pray. In this type of environment, the prayer center acts as a single location for the prayer meetings of the churches in the region.
   1. Para-church: Prayer Works, Ft. Wayne IN
   2. Local church: Great Southwest Prayer Center, Houston TX

G. **A Missions Base:**
   This is where 24/7 prayer is the core value. They are willing to invest at least 50% of their budget in building the House of Prayer through salaries, facilities and other resources devoted to the House of Prayer. They may not begin with 24/7 availability, but they continually take steps to get there. The House of Prayer is the main message and, while they may do other things, keeping the fire on the altar takes priority. They intend to become a 24/7 Missions hub for the Church in a city or region using a common model and sharing a common purpose. It has both a mandate and the grace to build a 24/7 reality led by teams and utilizes missions staff to run the ministry.

1. Local church: Gate City Church or IHOP Eastern Gate
2. Para-church: The Prayer Room DFW or Pasadena International HOP
3. Missions organization: YWAM Kona

H. Cross Culture:

There are a growing number of expressions of the House of Prayer springing up all over the world that are worth mentioning. We don't yet have much understanding on how these expressions work because so much of their infrastructure is so closely knit to their culture. They are clear indications that America doesn't own the market on what the House of Prayer can look like.
1. Prison watches: Argentina and South Africa
2. Prayer towers: Indonesia
3. Tribes with dedicated prayer huts: In remote places
4. Prayer mountains: South Korea
5. House of Prayer cell churches: Underground Church in China

Session Three: Mandates of a Missions Base

I. What is a Missions Base:

A missions base is a place where believers come to experience the Lord through prayer and worship and to be equipped with the necessary tools to navigate the difficulties of this generation (which we believe to be the last one).

A. Atmosphere of Enjoyable Prayer:

There is a real goal of having prayer burn like a furnace night and day 7 days a week where worshippers can come and enjoy His presence anytime in their schedules. Some come for refreshment, others for a peaceful place to study or read, and others still come just to get away from the rest of the intensity of life.

> *"I will bring to my holy mountain and give them joy in my house of prayer. Their burnt offerings and sacrifices will be accepted on my altar; for my house will be called a house of prayer for all nations" (Isaiah 56:7).*

B. A Service to God:

These ministries exist to facilitate enjoyable prayer with the main focus being a ministry to God first and then people secondly. Christ Himself said that the greatest commandment was to love the Lord our God with all our heart, soul and strength and then secondly to love our neighbors. With this in mind, teams are put in place to serve with worship and praise as the Levites did.

> *"Teacher, which is the greatest commandment in the Law?" Jesus replied: "'Love the Lord your God with all your heart and with all your soul and with all your mind.' This is the first and greatest commandment. And the second is like it: 'Love your neighbor as yourself.' All the Law and the Prophets hang on these two commandments" (Matthew 22:36-40).*

C. A Priesthood Before Man:

The missions base also acts as a priesthood where the people intercede on behalf of the city and the people that live there. Everyone involved shares the responsibility to keep the prayer furnace burning night and day before the Lord.

> "*The fire on the altar must be kept burning; it must not go out. Every morning the priest is to add firewood and arrange the burnt offering on the fire and burn the fat of the fellowship offerings on it*" (Leviticus 6:12).

II. Gleaning from the Missions Base Concept:

A. Contrast and Overlap:

Depending on where you land in the process of defining your expression, this session will serve you in various ways. The mandates of a missions base and the calling for a prayer group that meets for an hour each day at your local church may look quite different, but there will be some overlap. Whatever the case you can certainly draw ideas from the way a missions base operates.

B. Evolving into a Missions Base:

It is also noteworthy that some missions bases will evolve over time and may start off quite small only to grow into these mandates over time. That has been our story; we began in a living room in 2005 doing 14 prayer meetings a week, and then over time we added hours, grew in number and expanded our infrastructure. While we were wholly unable to fulfill any of these mandates at our start, they were things that we were thinking and talking about; they were goals and things we planned to take steps toward. As unique and costly as each of these mandates are, it was essential that we began making strides toward these things in intentional ways even from our formative years.

C. Aspects of the Mandate:

Below I have listed some of the foundational assignments which will be the focus of this session. These are grown into over time and not typically birthed overnight, so a ministry may still be considered a missions base even if these haven't yet reached their fullness but are well underway.

1. Establish literal 24/7 prayer
2. All hours led by live worship teams
3. Be run by full time missionary staff
4. Bless the region with servant hearted leadership
5. Become a regional training center

Session 3: Mandates of a Missions Base

D. At the Seven Year Mark:
1. What things have looked like for us:
   At seven years into our journey, The Prayer Room was 14/7 with live worship (that's just a little over the halfway mark). Our teams were mostly small or led by a single worship leader. Our staff was small with only 5 full timers and 2 part timers. We filled in the blanks with about 15 more volunteer staff and then a small army of others involved in our community. We were doing our best to serve the prayer movement in the region, mostly by praying for all the ministries and ministers that we have come in contact with (we had two prayer meetings per week committed to them). As for a regional training center, the infrastructure is there, but not too many people attend it. A few came each semester and we really do offer some valuable training. There was just not a lot of participation.
2. Beauty of faithfulness:
   There is a beauty in the smallness of all this…as we're still doing it. The principle that we are banking on, that we have seen the Lord affirm time and time again, is to be faithful with little and then He will give you more.
3. We're a missions base:
   So, we're a missions base, and I've considered us to be a missions base from the time we had 3 daily prayer meetings, a dedicated building and our first full time staff member (me).

III. Blessing to Your City:

A. Powerful Effects of Your Presence in the Region:
1. Helps to unify the Church across denominations (Jn. 17:23-24)
2. Perpetual prayer will bring revival to your city (Ac. 2:42-47)
3. Jesus' worth is proclaimed in a lavish way (Re. 5:9)
4. You provide a profound light in the darkness (Eph. 5:8)

B. Goals for the Place of Prayer:
1. To present the Father with perpetual praise and adoration (Le. 6:12)
2. To create a place where God's ear is attentive (2Ch. 7:14-15)
3. To contend for God's Kingdom objectives to be accomplished (Mt. 6:9-10)

C. Ways a Missions Base Serves the Church:
1. Provides a place of prayer for the people of the city (Ac. 16:13)
2. See the sick and the hurting healed (Jm. 5:15)

HOW TO BUILD A HOUSE OF PRAYER

      3. Usher in God's tangible presence into that city (2Ch. 7:2-3)
      4. Offers a unique training environment (Da. 11:35)

D. Creation of A Godly Community:
      1. A wholehearted people that spurs one another on in righteousness
      2. A community of encouraging likeminded believers
      3. A broader context of spiritual family and kingdom friendships

E. Prayer Focuses:
      1. Empower area ministries to do the work of the Kingdom (Eph. 6:18)
      2. Pray in the harvest (Jn. 3:16)
      3. Praying for workers to be released (Mt. 9:37-38)
      4. Praying for justice (Lk. 18:1, 7-8)
      5. Praying for the unity of the Church (Ro. 15:5)

IV. Mandates Pertaining to Worship and Prayer:

A. A Prayer Ministry for Jesus:
      1. A place to declare His worth
      2. A place where His desires are interceded for
      3. A place where people encounter Him

B. 24/7 Prayer:
Missions bases carry the unique mandate to form literal night and day prayer furnaces that operate 24/7. This means expanding hours into 24 hours a day, 7 days a week, 365 days a year.

C. Live Worship:
The element of live worship is essential to sustaining the night and day element of the mandate. It helps to keep people engaged in a way like nothing else that we have control over (temperature, atmosphere, volume, etc.). This requires lots of singers and musicians which have to be trained and organized into teams.

D. Full Time Missionaries:
Missions base also means having full and part time staff who raise their own support as missionaries in order to give themselves in a focused way to this God-initiated mission.

Session 3: Mandates of a Missions Base

1. Without full time staff:
   It is nearly impossible to keep things going in a continual manner without people who can give their full attention to the organizing and maintaining of the prayer meetings. An intercessory missionary is one who has committed to prayer and fasting as the first work of ministry with a view to establishing a 24-hour canopy of prayer that will help to make outreach more anointed and effective for the church in your region.
2. New paradigm:
   This is a new paradigm of mission work that God is initiating. For quite some time most ministry work has centered on the Second Commandment; reaching out to the world with the love of God. However, for the work of the Second Commandment to be effective and anointed, it should be accomplished by individuals whose hearts are alive and passionate in intimacy through experiencing the reality of the First Commandment; loving the Lord God with all your heart, mind, soul and strength. It is essential that we purpose to restore the First Commandment to first place. With the First Commandment in first place, hearts are energized in love. Outreach to the lost then becomes a natural overflow of a life that is soaring in intimacy with God.
3. Support raising:
   Intercessory missionaries are supported through partner development and financial support. An intercessory missionary is the modern-day equivalent of a Levite in the Tabernacle of David (who was fully supported to do his work).

V. Mandates for the People:

A. A Refuge for Hurting People:
1. A place of refreshment for the weary
2. A place where the lonely can find a family
3. A place where the lost/demonized/sick can find healing

B. Servant-Hearted Leadership:
Missions bases need a clear vision to help in whatever ways able to see night and day prayer birthed and sustained all across their region. This may come in the form of praying for, encouraging and helping resource prayer groups across the city or state. Servant leadership in your city is a major part of God's plan for the expansion of the prayer movement. This may also include planting houses of prayer and praying churches in the future.

C. **Regional Training Center:**
   In order to see all of this accomplished, it is important to begin strategizing how to evolve into full and part time programs such as internships, Bible school, etc. to help fuel and fund the operation of a full-time missions base.
   1. A place that declares the hour we are living in
   2. A place that instructs about God's affections
   3. A place that trains up forerunner messengers

UNIT II

Leading

Session 4: The Call to Build God's House

Session 5: Building Your Team

Session 6: Things to Embrace and Things to Avoid

Session Four: The Call to Build God's House

I. The Lord Desires that His House be Built:

> This is what the LORD Almighty says: "Give careful thought to your ways. <u>Go up into the mountains and bring down timber and build the house, so that I may take pleasure in it</u> and be honored," says the LORD" (Haggai 1:7-8).

> "<u>I have posted</u> watchmen on your walls, O Jerusalem; they will never be silent day or night. You who call on the LORD, <u>give yourselves no rest</u>, and give him no rest till he establishes Jerusalem and makes her the praise of the earth" (Isaiah 62:6-7).

> "After this <u>I will return and rebuild David's fallen tent</u>. Its ruins I will rebuild, and I will restore it, that the remnant of men may seek the Lord, and all the Gentiles who bear my name, says the Lord, who does these things' that have been known for ages" (Acts 15:16-18).

II. God is Building and So Must We:

A. The Lord's Essential Involvement:

> Unless the LORD builds the house, its builders labor in vain. Unless the LORD watches over the city, the watchmen stand guard in vain (Psalm 127:1).

B. Unless there are Laborers:

For some time when I looked at this passage I focused on the supernatural intervention of the Lord, which is absolutely essential if the house is to be built. But one day while I was studying, I felt the Lord give me some divine commentary on the verse. I felt that He told me that though it was true that if He wasn't building the house its laborers labored in vain, that if the laborers didn't labor then there would be no house. This shifted my thinking to understand how important it is that we labor; that is, work very hard. Though it is a house of prayer it will not be built without hard work, long hours, and strategic thinking.

C. David's Exhortation to Do the Work:

"All this," David said, "I have in writing from the hand of the LORD upon me, and he gave me understanding in all the details of the plan." David also said to Solomon his son, "<u>Be strong and courageous, and do the work</u>. Do not be afraid or discouraged, for the LORD God, my God, is with you. <u>He will not fail you or forsake you until all the work for the service of the temple of the LORD is finished</u>. The divisions of the priests and Levites are ready for all the work on the temple of God, and every willing man skilled in any craft will help you in all the work. The officials and all the people will obey your every command" (1 Chronicles 28:19-21).

III. Common Leadership Mistakes:

As leaders commissioned to build the House of Prayer, we have a very clear path on how to move forward. Unfortunately, many become distracted by not keeping their eyes on some very simple objectives.

A. Objective One—Begin:

Don't talk about prayer, do it. As your number one priority begin having regular prayer meetings. I know too many people who talk about prayer but never actually pray.

B. Objective Two—Maintain:

Refuse to let up on the prayer meetings you begin. You will have every reason in the world to back off, don't.

C. Objective Three—Expand:

You have to keep it at the top of your priorities to continually add prayer meetings to your schedule. It is just as easy to become stagnant and cease the building process as the temptation was not to begin in the first place, or to give up when it got hard.

D. Have a Plan—Work Your Plan:

When it comes down to the mechanics of what makes a house of prayer either work or not work, things can be summed up very simply; does the leader have a plan for the ministry and is that leader actually taking the steps on his/her plan?

IV. Foundational Importance of Your Efforts:

If God is calling you to build a HOP, then you as a leader actually have to be in the meetings. At the start you need to be in pretty much all of them, because as fragile of a thing as this is, it can easily fall apart.

Session 4: The Call to Build God's House

A. Your Time Investment:
Settle it now; this is going to take a lot of our time and energy to build. We must set ourselves for the long haul, thinking about the House of Prayer in terms of decades not years.

All hard work brings a profit, but mere talk leads only to poverty (Proverbs 14:23).

Therefore, my dear brothers, stand firm. Let nothing move you. Always give yourselves fully to the work of the Lord, because you know that your labor in the Lord is not in vain (1Corinthians 15:58).

B. Being an Unmovable Leader:
Establishing prayer takes time, and it takes at least one person who is absolutely unmovable even if it means they are the only one in the room. You, as the leader, are setting the example and the pace for what everyone will follow. The Enemy will launch all of his arsenal at you, but if God has called you then you are also equipped to withstand his attacks of discouragement, disillusionment, distraction and perhaps most painful of all, the small beginnings that remain small for some time. This is the crucible which God uses to raise up leadership after His own heart.

C. Coordinate According to Your Schedule:
Set up a prayer meeting schedule around what you yourself can attend and remain faithful to it for the long haul. Do not make the mistake of basing your decision mainly off of what people claim they will commit to. Of course you want to consider the input of those around you, but ultimately the issue of the schedule rests on what you will be able to commit to and uphold.

1. Stay committed:
   We as leaders must stay committed to our committed time in prayer and must be the backbone of the prayer schedule.
2. Pass up opportunities:
   No matter what else comes up as opportunities for the ministry, we need to keep prayer meetings the priority.
3. Do what you say:
   If we advertise certain hours of operation, then it is important that we actually do what we claim.

V. Foundational Building Principles:
A. Build with Predictability:
1. Pray at the same time each day:

Especially when you are starting off, the most efficient way to build your prayer schedule is to be predictable. If you begin with evening prayer meetings, then start them at the same time every day or at least M-F (example 7:00PM-8:00PM). If you decide to start off with a morning meeting, then do it daily at the same time five or seven days a week (example 6:00AM-7:00AM).
2. Ease of communication:
You want your prayer schedule to be as easy to communicate as possible. You have enough hindrances in explaining your ministry for them not to have the added difficulty of remembering when you meet. Make it easy for people to get involved.
3. Arranging your personal life:
It is invaluable in developing a prayer culture where people can begin to build their life around the prayer meetings. You will also find this crucial for yourself as a leader as you attempt to build the ever so intrusive dynamic of adding regular prayer meetings into the schedule of your own personal life.
4. Developing your ethos:
The same set time every day gives your community something to rally around whether it's morning, noon or night, while scattered meetings make for an unnecessarily difficult environment. This is the same reason why businesses have regular hours of operation instead of random time slots that they are open. Whatever you decide will develop some of your community's culture.

B. Create a Simple Model:

To maintain prayer meetings long term, you are going to need some sort of model. Truth be told, not all of your meetings will be fun or energized, and you will absolutely need something for people to follow as a default. Your model can vary greatly based off of a number of factors. The point is to try and identify a general way that the meetings will flow. Leave room for the Spirit to move, but have a plan; you will be grateful more times than not that you had a default direction to go.
1. Prayer focus
2. Amount of time allotted for your prayer meetings
3. Resources at your disposal
4. Whether you have worship leaders, singers or musicians
5. Number of people in your meetings
6. Tenure and maturity level of those involved

C. Ask People to Commit to Specific Meetings:

You may choose to call it something different, but the essence is the same; that is, a set prayer schedule that people sign up for specific shifts and make a commitment to be in attendance at those times each week. We call this commitment "The Sacred Trust" and we make sure to keep it at the forefront of what we do as a ministry. This is the only way you can build prayer with any measure of reliability because there are people who have said they will be there in the room to make sure a prayer meeting happens. As soon as you begin regular prayer meetings, you want to start recruiting people to commit to individual prayer shifts.

D. Adapt as You Go:
In the first 3 months of doing daily prayer meetings, you will learn so much about yourself, about human psychology and about what works and doesn't. Take what you learn and adapt. You may find that your prayer model needs some tweaking, that some additional guidelines about attendance may be helpful and that the topics you picked were all wrong. Adapt. The great thing about daily prayer meetings that you are the one giving leadership to is that you can always improve them and tailor them to your needs and the needs of your community.

VI. Build According to Plan:
No prayer ministry starts off looking like how it will end up, but it does have the DNA of what it will be even at its conception. The point of detailing what the different expressions look like was to help paint a picture for where you are headed and what you are aiming for. We want to have an idea of what we are building so that we can be sure to invest our energies and establish infrastructure where our efforts won't be lost along the way. We want to build according to plan.

Session Five: Building Your Team

I. Intro:

While we do leadership development in the traditional sense here, this session isn't about the 5 steps to good leadership. The focus of this session really has far more to do with helping us find ways to get people involved in a committed way and developing good methods of building a team of intercessors and worshipers that take ownership of the ministry together.

II. Strategies for Enlisting Help:

Below are suggestions that have worked here at The Prayer Room and that we have found to be common practices at the larger successful houses of prayer across the nation. The terms may vary from place to place, but the concepts are staples at ministries like PIHOP in Los Angeles, Gate City Church in Atlanta, IHOP Eastern Gate in New Jersey and other successful houses of prayer.

A. Sacred Trust:

I strongly suggest establishing a way to distinguish between visitors and community based off of their commitment to the vision. Being part of the community means that a person is willing to commit to at least one prayer shift a week with you. At TPR we call this the Sacred Trust, and it is the foundation of how we build all of our prayer meetings.

B. Prayer Leaders:

Get people to commit to leading a particular prayer set. Maybe it's a topic they feel connected to, or maybe it's just a hole you have and really need someone to step in and fill. Either way this gets another person committed to prayer meetings and serving the vision of the house. Your prayer leaders will begin to take ownership of the ministry because you let them have part in it. After your model grows a bit, then you

can start recruiting people to other designated roles on the team.
1. Worship leader
2. Assistant prayer leader
3. Musicians
4. Singers
5. Ushers

C. **Core Leadership:**
Depending on the circumstance, you may or may not have your key leaders at the onset. Perhaps it's even best to wait a few months after you have begun daily prayer meetings (even 5 days a week) to find out who is really with you. But one thing that is important is that if they are going to be on the leadership of a prayer ministry, then they need to be committed to more prayer meetings than what is the common expectation. We lead by example. A suggestion may be if you are wanting non leaders to commit to 2 sets a week, then have your core leadership commit to 4 sets a week. Below I've listed of the reasons this is important.
1. Setting the example:
    People in the ministry need to see their leaders are actually praying.
2. Actually cultivating a prayer life:
    Our core leadership needs time to cultivate and work out their prayer life in God, which is by no means an automatic thing.
3. Being around:
    We want our leaders around regularly to help greet new people, build relationships, answer questions and put out fires.

D. **Volunteer Staff:**
Next level of involvement is for those wanting to get more connected but who don't have 20 hours a week to commit. Create a 6-8 hour a week version of involvement, which mostly means more prayer meetings, while it allows them to play a specific role in the functioning of the ministry. Below is an example of what this commitment level could look like.
1. Specific prayer commitment:
    A commitment to 4 hours of prayer each week
2. Unique role:
    Give them responsibility over something the ministry needs; it could be as simple as visitor follow-up.
3. Corporate meeting:

Session 5: Building Your Team

Have them commit to participate in your weekly service.

E. Paid Staff:
Having full time and part time staff makes the world of difference in the operations of a prayer ministry. Not only are they available to help with all the administrative needs, but because they are paid, your requirement for how many prayer meetings they would be in is much higher than a volunteer.

F. Any Warm Body:
All the above suggestions make for more warm bodies in more prayer meetings which means greater capacity to grow the schedule. People making commitments to prayer meetings is the essential building block for sustaining prayer long term.

III. Principles to Operate By:

A. Leading by Example:
As stated before, we as leaders must actually be living lifestyles of prayer ourselves or we cannot call people to it. In the same way, we need to live example lives for our leaders to see and for our staff to model.

B. Promote According to Godliness not Giftedness:
The best way to create jealousy is to promote people merely off of their gifting or skill set. This will always cause the wrong people to stay and the right people to look for the door. Instead, we need to look for godly character.
1. Faithfulness
2. Servant attitude
3. Work ethic
4. Positive presence and don't complain
5. Sincerity
6. Tenure with you (obviously in conjunction to the above)

C. Softening the Heavy Yoke:
You may find that the only way to take steps and to get things done is to ask people to commit to a lot. This doesn't have to be your downfall, but there are some principles that need to be at play.
1. Lift a finger to help the people.

> *Then Jesus said to the crowds and to his disciples: "The teachers of the law and the Pharisees sit in Moses' seat. So you must obey them and do everything they tell you. <u>But do not do what they do, for they do not practice what they preach</u>. They tie up heavy loads and put them on men's shoulders, <u>but they themselves are not willing to lift a finger to move them</u>" (Matthew 23:1-4).*

Jesus' issue wasn't necessarily the difficult work that had to be done, it was that the Pharisees didn't do anything to help carry the load that they assigned for others. Everyone wants a general who is right there with them in the trenches, while no one likes a leader who makes difficult demands and then props their feet up.

2. Love covers over a multitude of sins.

> *The end of all things is near. Therefore be clear minded and self-controlled so that you can pray. Above all, love each other deeply, because love covers over a multitude of sins (1Peter 4:7-8).*

Here Peter gives us divine insight into how to build prayer at the end of the age. He tells us that, in addition to ordering our lives so that we can pray, that we must love each other deeply.

IV. Team Building Initiatives:

Pressures are often intense and so it is important that your team likes each other and knows how to operate as a unit. All of the following are pretty self-explanatory but super valuable in building the bond of peace within the prayer environment.

A. Planning Fun Community Activities:

As discussed in the last session, these activities are important especially while things are small because they help give people a sense of identity to the ministry and they establish relationships that sustain the ministry.

B. Staff Training:

Providing ongoing training for your staff is important not only for their betterment, but also to continue to show them your commitment to invest in them.

C. Staff Meetings:

This regular time with just your staff allows you to communicate important information but powerfully establishes a team. Everyone in the room regularly gets to see who that team is and have a sense of doing something together.

D. Staff Retreats:

If you can pull it off, I highly recommend taking your staff out of town once a year

Session 5: Building Your Team

to re-bond and re-cast vision for where you are headed as a team. Our annual staff retreat is universally looked forward to by all, is relaxing, fun and only loosely structured. My goal is to get them out of their element and to fall in love with each other over the weekend as they play and eat together.

E. Staff Privileges:
We try to invent ways (mostly non-monetary ways) to treat our staff as special. They work so hard and have so few privileges that anywhere we can, we seek to bless them.
1. A staff-only break room
2. Give them a discount on paid activities (even just $5 less)
3. Let them have first pick or the best seats
4. Plan a special staff-only dinner

Session Six: Things to Embrace and Things to Avoid

I. Labor with Longsuffering:

A. Our Beginning:
When we first began to understand that the Lord was working in us to build the house of prayer, there were a number of conflicting realities that worked to keep us in the race. The first of which was that in my zeal, I committed to the Lord that we would do this prayer ministry until He returned; and the second was that I had absolutely no idea what that meant and the years of hard work that I had ahead of me.

B. A Call to Persevere:
I wrongly assumed that we would be 24/7 in a few years (I was thinking that 5 seemed like a long time) and that then we could sorta coast after that. As the months and years began to pass, however, I learned that while this was the most rewarding ministry endeavor I had ever embarked on, this was not going to be easy or fast. My heart was very much alive in the work, but I was working long hours and late nights in order to keep the difficult balance of staying in the place of prayer myself and running the administration to keep the doors open. It was tough.

C. Ten Years Before You Look Up:
Early on, I drew strength from a quote I heard from Mike Bickle about setting your face to the task and not looking up for at least a decade. The way he put it was to settle in and not consider your options until you've been doing it for at least ten years. Well, at present TPR is almost 7 years in and I'm glad that I never considered quitting as an option. I encourage you to really weigh whether the Lord is calling you to build His house, and if He is then settle it now that you're not coming up for air for a decade, then you can reassess and see if it's been worth it. I think you'll find that it has been.

II. Make Connections:

Relational connections take time and in most cases there isn't an immediate payoff. In fact sometimes the payoff is never tangible. It is however invaluable that you invest energy and time into relationships outside of your ministry; this will provide you with a number of benefits that may take some years to realize.

A. Network with Other Prayer Ministries:
1. Camaraderie:
   Sharing the journey, I have found that there is a unique bond I have with people who are building the house of prayer.
2. Share ideas:
   You will find that other prayer ministries are doing things that you can really learn from. Don't reinvent the wheel; if the ministry down the way is already doing something well, copy as much of it as makes sense for your context. Many things that we do at TPR are as a result of things that I learned from observing other prayer ministries.
3. Shared events:
   When it makes sense, do some small number of things collectively. It's fun to get everyone together to co-host a conference or event that strengthens the prayer movement as a whole across your region.
4. Consider joining forces:
   Sometimes, especially for small houses of prayer that are really struggling, the right thing is actually to join forces with another ministry so that the combined strength would be far greater than the two ministries separately. But you would never consider such a thing unless you knew each other and had grown to trust one another.

B. Connect with Our House of Prayer:
1. Contact person:
   Because we've been doing this since 2005 and have strong ties across the nation I recommend reaching out to us to find someone here who you can begin to build a relationship with. This doesn't have to be a senior leader in order to be helpful to your cause, in fact any of our staff is a great starting point.
2. Strike team:
   Often we are able to send a team to your city or house of prayer to help encourage and strengthen you. These trips are a very affordable way to get an injection from our staff as these short trips are often very impacting for you and your team.

Session 6: Things to Embrace and Things to Avoid

    3. Small conference:
    When you are ready (mostly this has to do with your administrative capacities and having at least a few people with you) consider having one of our leaders come for a small-scale conference. These are always helpful to the vision and morale of your community. We probably had about 20 people in our community the first time we did something of this nature.

C. **Connect with a Regional Missions Base:**
Somewhere in your part of the country there is a house of prayer that the Lord is highlighting as a regional missions base. We strongly encourage you to connect with them with intentionality. They can serve you in many ways that will be helpful to you.
    1. Learn from them:
    When you begin to relate to a small but established missions base, you are dealing with a ministry that has already had to work through and figure out many of the things you will soon face. Hearing how they have done things will save you time and give you ideas about how you should proceed.
    2. Draw resources from them:
    They will have resources that you don't have yet; things like teaching resources, prayer trainings and handouts. Additionally, they may be willing to share some of their in-house documents that help run the behind-the-scenes infrastructure; these types of resources are invaluable for you.
    3. Stay connected regionally:
    As a regional missions base, they will be connected with other prayer ministries in the area and have some resources that will be helpful to you. We know most of these places and these connections will be helpful to you as you grow.
    4. Participate in larger area events:
    By simply being connected to a regional missions base, you will be able to participate in the events they host which often draw from resources and connections you may not have access to. We see many smaller ministries from our region come and glean in this way, and their teams always leave strengthened.

D. **Connect with Church Leaders:**
It's important to form good relationships with the pastors and ministry leaders in your city, especially making connections with the leaders of those who attend your prayer meetings.
    1. Earn their confidence:

HOW TO BUILD A HOUSE OF PRAYER

Serve them, pray for them and speak well of them. Help the leaders in your area know that you are there to help them in the role the Lord gave them and to be a blessing.

2. Potential opportunities to present:

While you can't start off your relationship trying to make this happen, it is a fair hope that some of these relationships will allow for you to present the vision and value of the house of prayer down the road. This could even include being invited to speak to their congregation in some way. No pastor is going to just let any person come and speak to their people however, which is why relationship is so important.

3. Potential support:

Similarly, it's not wise to begin asking a leader for money when you first meet them, but it's reasonable that as a relationship forms you may be able to present the costs and benefits of the house of prayer to your ministry friends.

III. Avoid Conflict with Church Leaders:

Some conflicts with area leaders will be unavoidable because of the very nature of what you are doing and what you believe. But I've found that many conflicts are unnecessary and occur because we just didn't put forth the effort to avoid the problems. There are three main ways that you can honor the area leaders to gain their confidence in you and begin to build good rapport. The points below are especially true of para-church expressions of the house of prayer, but they certainly apply to how you should relate to other area leaders with regard to their people who are attending your meetings regardless of your expression.

A. Support their Tithing:

Good or bad, it takes finances to run a ministry, and the pastor down the street has costs he is looking at which include his salary. You really want to navigate this issue well so as to avoid becoming enemies with leaders in your region. If you take up offerings at your house of prayer, or if you have a donations box, then post or regularly announce that you want to make sure people know to give to their local church first.

B. Support their Church Attendance:

My experience over the years is that people who claim to be believers but are not involved in a local church have a number of issues that they need to work through. At The Prayer Room we actually require that people get involved and remain involved

Session 6: Things to Embrace and Things to Avoid

at a local church instead of considering their attendance in a prayer meeting as their only means of connection to the Body of Christ. Pastors like this. It shows that you support what they are doing, that the house of prayer isn't some rogue ministry for all the discontented to hang out, but that instead it supports the local church.

C. Support the Pastor When there is a Schedule Conflict:
People are going to have schedule conflicts between your house of prayer and their local church. My suggestion is lose, lose and lose every time. Don't even begin down the road for fighting for their priorities when it comes to their church involvement. That pastor is doing his best to organize his ministry and to create things to help his people; don't stand in the way of that. We always tell the people who come around The Prayer Room: "If ever there is a conflict between something for your local church and something at TPR, your local church wins every time. Make sure to get a replacement and take care that your responsibilities are met, but please go do the local church thing."

IV. Avoid Unnecessary Financial Costs:

A. Building Costs
Meet someplace free. There is no reason you should have to pay a dollar in building costs until you have grown to a point where you can support that. People add unnecessary financial burdens to themselves by trying to start off with a nice place, or a dedicated space. The space isn't the ministry, the prayer meetings are, and you can pray anywhere. So don't throw any money at rental space until you have to; in the meantime meet in a living room or someone's office or a small room in the back of the church.

B. Promotions:
While I recommend having a website and some inexpensive promotional materials, some ministries spend too much too soon. Truth of the matter is that until you have bunch of prayer meetings going, a bit of growth and some infrastructure in place, all the promotions in the world won't really work. Build your ministry before you spend a bunch of time and money promoting it; make sure it's actually something you want people to see.

C. Events:
There is no reason why you have to spend more than a few dollars on your events for

quite some time. For years we did our events in my living room and our costs were limited to paper and snacks. Don't go into debt trying to pull off something bigger than you are ready for. Do events that match your sphere of influence.

V. Don't Ignore Visitors:

The visitor you have today may well be your next servant hearted worship leader down the road; you just don't know. But if you aren't careful with your visitors, you may pass up some phenomenal people who really would have gotten plugged in with your ministry.

A. Give Them Your Attention:

Especially while you are small, every visitor is your most precious commodity, make sure you are personally making time to chat with them and hear a bit about them. It's always a fair question to ask how they heard about your prayer ministry and what they thought of your meeting.

B. Train Your People:

It's not enough for you to connect with them, but that is an excellent starting point. You need to instruct your regulars to be very visitor aware and visitor focused. This is not natural for most people, but if visitors come in and no one takes time to talk with them, most will not come back.

C. Have a Follow Up System:

Get their information while they are with you. We recommend a simple email sign up sheet. Then have someone follow up with them that week. It's important that they are personally contacted and that it happens within just days of their visit. We used to assign our regulars to ask each visitor out to coffee just to make sure someone showed them that we cared.

VI. Be Careful Not to Burn the People Out:

It takes a driven leader to build the house of prayer. In fact my experience has been unless the leader is constantly pushing things forward, prayer loses its priority in the people's lives and the house of prayer eventually ceases to be altogether. It's absolutely necessary to set expectations and to call the people to press on, but the tendency is to push too hard. This is a delicate dance because too little and you lose ground and too much and you burn the people out, and ultimately you don't have anyone left to push. I've listed a few of the common pitfalls that can end up burning people out if you aren't careful.

Session 6: Things to Embrace and Things to Avoid

A. Trying to Grow Too Fast:
Some will attempt to grow their prayer ministries by adding too many prayer sets too quickly, faster than the community can really keep up with. This comes from a deep desire to see the work go forth, but we must always remember that the work of God is built with weak human beings. It is necessary that we give careful consideration before implementing steps that require more from them to fulfill. Alternatively, we don't want to allow our efforts not to burn people out to become excuses to never push the vision forward and add prayer sets and support structure.

B. Overworking the People:
Overloading people with administrative responsibilities is another way to get them to quit. Everyone can handle a little, in fact the family concept, which the Kingdom of God is built on, requires that everyone has a role and does his or her part. But the tendency of leaders is to push too hard and to give people more to do than is wisdom for them to uphold. Remember they have jobs and lives and families and other responsibilities, so be careful not to give people too much. We have two suggestions with regard to avoiding this pitfall; one is to give your volunteers responsibilities that they can complete in an hour or less per week. And the second is to do some measure of follow-up to see that they are actually only working about that much. It's human nature to people-please, and there is a good chance that an assignment that you thought would only take a short amount of time is in reality costing them late nights and long hours that are secretly frustrating them.

C. Imbalanced Teaching:
Because at The Prayer Room we have such a strong emphasis on the end times, we have had to be creative in making sure to provide some balance on messages such as God's love and the pursuit of intimate relationship with Jesus. If your message is all intensity and no resting in the Lord, then people will get heavy hearted and it will be difficult to sustain. We do lots of devotional worship sets as well as worship with the word each week, all of which focus on the love of God and our wholehearted yet weak love back to Him, while we only teach on the intensity of the end time message at most for an hour each week. If you are all "revival" and "pay the price in intercession" and "go hard after God" without a good dose of "how He loves us" you are positioning yourself for burnout.

D. Pay Attention:
Just pay attention to where people are at. Ask your regulars how they are doing and

try to keep your finger on the pulse of what's going on. One person feeling overwhelmed may not be cause for alarm, but pay attention to trends and make necessary changes to help the overall health of your community.

VII. Watch Yourself as a Leader:

Every leader is confronted with the below pitfalls at some point or another, but no one has to succumb to them. It's been my experience, unfortunately, that many get stuck in one or more of these avoidable hang-ups and so the ministry is negatively impacted.

A. Personal Discouragement:

If you are not intentional to cast and recast vision for yourself about why you are doing what you are doing, then you will become discouraged easily. Build in vision casting resources into your regular diet so that you're never long since your last dose of reminder. It's easy to just set our nose to the grind and forget why we are doing this. Be intentional to recast vision for yourself regularly. Below are some ways to do so.

1. Journal the things the Lord has spoken to you
2. Spend a prayer meeting just asking the Lord to re-envision you
3. Listen to IHOP-KC's Encountering Jesus series
4. Do a study on the scriptures related to the end time prayer movement

B. Quitting:

The devil wants every one of you to quit. He hates you and he hates the work you are doing. He will cause you many heartaches and blockades and sets backs.

1. When it all goes south:

    Just know that going into it so when all your leaders quit the same month, your preaching seems fruitless and you can't get ahead financially, you don't consider it odd.

    Dear friends, do not be surprised at the painful trial you are suffering, as though something strange were happening to you. But rejoice that you participate in the sufferings of Christ, so that you may be overjoyed when his glory is revealed (1Peter 4:12-13).

2. Don't quit, just press on.

    Therefore, since we are surrounded by such a great cloud of witnesses, let us throw off everything that hinders and the sin that so easily entangles. And let us run with perseverance the race marked out for us... (Hebrews 12:1).

Session 6: Things to Embrace and Things to Avoid

C. Losing Your Oil:

If you find yourself working during your prayer meetings instead of trying to connect with the Lord, it's only time before you run out of oil (Mt. 25:1-13). This is pretty easy to fall into because there is always more work to do than there are hours to get it done. You have to draw some firm lines for yourself so that you don't lose your way in the Lord. What's it all worth at the end if the vessels that the Lord appointed to lead the prayer ministry (you) are burned out and unconnected to Him?

D. Tendency to Back Off:

When things get tough, there is a strong tendency to back off and take steps backwards. Personally I believe that there are ways around this in almost every instance, and further, I know that this is the desire of the enemy for your ministry to shrink up and wither away. If you stay healthy as a spiritual leader and submitted to His plans, then you shouldn't have to go backwards though you really may well have to trim things up significantly. We just recently went through a season of severe pruning at The Prayer Room. Before it started, we had about 100 people committed to prayer meetings and by the time it was over we were down to under 70, but we kept the same amount of prayer meetings. We did however have to downgrade many of the teams to single person devotional worship sets (which are great). We had to trim some support programs in order to be able to focus all our attention on the main thing…prayer and worship to King Jesus. Let's never lose track of that point, and when it's time to cut things, let's cut programs not prayer.

E. Jealousy of Other Ministries:

As the prayer movement grows, there will be more and more houses of prayer pop up all over the place. It is important that we celebrate these expressions instead of becoming adversarial with them. The Lord wants prayer everywhere, in every place and in every congregation, so rejoice over what God is up to so that you don't fall into the trap of jealousy.

> *…there should be no division in the body, but that its parts should have equal concern for each other. If one part suffers, every part suffers with it; if one part is honored, every part rejoices with it (1Corinthians 12:25-26).*

UNIT III

Laying a Foundation

Session 7: Casting & Keeping the Vision

Session 8: Growth Strategies

Session 9: A Basic Prayer Model

Session Seven: Casting & Keeping the Vision

I. Calling People to the Vision:

Regular prayer meetings are rigorous to uphold in our culture because so little is asked of anyone from any angle. If you as the head leader do not clearly present and then continue to keep the vision before the people, they will not have the sustaining grace to stay steady through the years.

> *Where there is no revelation, the people cast off restraint (Proverbs 28:19 NIV).*
> *Where there is no vision, the people perish (Proverbs 28:19 KJV).*

II. The Four Heart Standards:

The below are the pillars that God gave Mike Bickle in 1982 as the DNA of the coming Prayer Movement. These were not given only to IHOP Kansas City but were intended to be blueprints for the movement at large. Significant promises of blessing, favor, strength and endurance have been tied to these often-neglected heart standards. Though you may call them different things and may approach them from slightly different angles, it is my suggestion that any person endeavoring to build a prayer furnace implement these four principles as foundation of what you're doing.

A. Intercession:

Not only intercessory prayer, but devotional prayer, worship, thanksgiving, and waiting upon the Lord. This heart standard is meant to communicate prayer as a lifestyle and necessity of literal 24/7 prayer. We strive to establish it and then maintain it once it is in place.

> *And pray in the Spirit on all occasions with all kinds of prayers and requests. With this in mind, be alert and always keep on praying for all the saints (Ephesians 6:18).*

B. Holiness:

Holding to purity, repentance, and the biblical standards of righteousness. This doesn't mean that we will never mess up, but it does mean that we commit to calling our shortcomings sin and that we confess them and turn from them. We commit to cultivate a community that thinks this way, teaches this way and lives this way.

Make every effort to live in peace with all men and to be holy; without holiness no one will see the Lord (Hebrews 12:14).

C. Offerings:

Radical giving. As Americans we are the richest group of people the world has ever seen, with the poorest amongst us having more than most of the world's population. We commit as a ministry to sow into the kingdom and to continually call the community into sacrificial giving. We believe that 10% is only the beginning point of our giving and that we should take less for ourselves so that we can give more.

Whoever sows sparingly will also reap sparingly, and whoever sows generously will also reap generously. Each man should give what he has decided in his heart to give, not reluctantly or under compulsion, for God loves a cheerful giver. And God is able to make all grace abound to you, so that in all things at all times, having all that you need, you will abound in every good work (2Corinthians 9:6-8).

D. Prophecy:

This speaks of both the subjective and the written Word of the Lord. We take prophecy seriously. It is the backbone of why we do what we are doing, and it is our sustainer when things get difficult. Prophecy motivates us to keep going. The subjective Word has both birthed this ministry and directed it via the Lord's Voice, dreams, visions, etc. The written Word reveals that great Tribulation is coming to the Earth in, what we believe to be, this generation. This has greatly set and stabilized our direction as a ministry, and is the foundational premise behind our training and existence as a missions base.

He said to them, "How foolish you are, and how slow of heart to believe all that the prophets have spoken!" (Luke. 24:25).

E. More Than These:

We certainly believe more than these four things, but these are our main focuses, and they are four areas that have received significant neglect but that we believe the Lord is highlighting in this hour. By taking on the difficulty and stigma of these 4 standards, our ministry powerfully benefits the local churches in this region.

Session 7: Casting & Keeping the Vision

III. Calling People to Specific Mandates:

A. Main and the Plain:
1. Obviously you are going to focus on prayer. This in itself is quite an undertaking, and if it is the only mandate we have as a ministry we will be very busy. Calling people to lifestyles of prayer is difficult. (Well, it's not hard to say it; the hard part is getting people to actually do it.) Even the ones that say yes to it will need constant reminders and encouragement as our flesh wars against us and our hearts prove to be mysteriously rebellious.
2. As leaders we need real clarity about "the why" behind prayer so that we can be vision casting machines able to ignite again those close to us that need a little reminder in the midst of the storms of life.

B. Knowing What the Lord has Given You:
You want to get some clarity on the unique aspects or initiatives that the Lord has given to your house that vary from the common mandate of prayer. This can include specific justice initiatives that you are to give energy to; it could be having a real focus on healing or a unique role in raising up other prayer ministries. The point is that you as the human leader want to identify what these things are so that you can cast the vision for them and then call people to it.

C. Don't Do Too Much Too Fast:
A mistake we can all make is spreading ourselves too thin. The Lord will often give us more vision than we have the capacity to pull off. This is a purposeful effort on His part to get us to carry certain things in our heart for years before it's time to launch them. If we are not careful we can have the right "what" but mess up the "when" and find ourselves doing too much too fast. By spreading ourselves thin like this, we burn people out, set ourselves up to disappoint others and slow the growth of the things that we really were to be focusing on that season. A time comes for those desires that are in our heart (or the hearts of those underneath us) to come to pass, but in the meantime we need to focus energy on doing well the things that we are already doing. We need to learn to discern what the Lord wants for our ministry in each season and for the timing of specific initiatives. The right thing at the wrong time is the wrong thing.

"Suppose one of you wants to build a tower. Will he not first sit down and estimate

the cost to see if he has enough money to complete it? For if he lays the foundation and is not able to finish it, everyone who sees it will ridicule him, saying, 'This fellow began to build and was not able to finish.'" (Luke 14:28-30).

D. Don't Do What He Called Someone Else to Do:

Simply put, as a ministry don't do someone else's part. God called you to prayer. In some sovereign way somehow He made you think that starting a prayer ministry was a good idea and that you should give yourself to it. He has that same power to speak to His servants regarding every single initiative of His heart. Don't take on extra initiatives. While valuable and I'm sure part of the broad work of the great commission, if they aren't things God has specifically called your ministry to undertake, then you will actually be using energy that was intended for what He has spoken to you about. Too many ministries try to do too much; in fact they try to do everything. We have the tendency to copy cat what the ministry next door is doing giving little thought to whether that's actually what the Lord wants for us to be doing.

I planted the seed, Apollos watered it, but God made it grow. So neither he who plants nor he who waters is anything, but only God, who makes things grow. The man who plants and the man who waters have one purpose, and each will be rewarded according to his own labor. For we are God's fellow workers; you are God's field, God's building (1Corinthians 3:6-9).

IV. Core Vision Motivators:

Getting involved is very different from staying involved. What has absolutely been the major factor for keeping/losing people's involvement has been a matter of whether they had and kept vision.

A. Urgency:

The End Times message is essential to motivating people into the urgency of the hour in which we live. This is a foundational aspect of vision that should not be overlooked no matter what your former theological position has been. The scriptures speak extensively about the great and terrible day of the Lord and how the only solution for mankind will be corporate prayer meetings crying out to God.

The end of all things is near. Therefore be clear minded and self-controlled so that you can pray (1Peter 4:7).

"Be careful, or your hearts will be weighed down with dissipation, drunkenness and the anxieties of life, and that day will close on you unexpectedly like a trap. For it will come upon all those who live on the face of the whole earth. Be always on the

Session 7: Casting & Keeping the Vision

watch, and pray that you may be able to escape all that is about to happen, and that you may be able to stand before the Son of Man" (Luke 21:34-36).

B. Intimacy:

The primary issue of our identity is knowing Christ and understanding how He feels about us. The Greatest Commandment is to love the Lord our God with our all. When we put these two concepts together—loving God and receiving His love for us—we unlock powerful dynamics of the heart which enables people to continue to connect with God in the place of prayer. Without this invaluable aspect of the message, people quickly lose vision for why they should keep coming to prayer meetings.

"Teacher, which is the greatest commandment in the Law?" Jesus replied: "Love the Lord your God with all your heart and with all your soul and with all your mind.' This is the first and greatest commandment" (Matthew 22:36-38).

"<u>Dark am I, yet lovely</u>, O daughters of Jerusalem, dark like the tents of Kedar, like the tent curtains of Solomon. Do not stare at me because I am dark, because I am darkened by the sun" (Song of Solomon 1:5-6).

"For your Maker is your husband—the LORD Almighty is his name—the Holy One of Israel is your Redeemer; he is called the God of all the earth" (Isaiah 54:5).

C. Worth of Christ:

We must continually revisit the vision of Christ' incomparable worth found all throughout scripture if we hope to have intercessors sustain the rigors of prayer long term. When our flesh is screaming at us, we need to have an anchor much stronger than the blowing wind. His worth is that stabilizing reality; inalterable and unchallenged by our circumstances. A community of believers that is rooted in His worth is able to withstand many pressures and inconveniences that otherwise there might not be sufficient inner strength to resist.

And they sang a new song: "You are worthy to take the scroll and to open its seals, because you were slain, and with your blood you purchased men for God from every tribe and language and people and nation" (Revelation 5:9).

D. The Prayer Movement:

Somehow we as humans draw great strength from knowing that we are not alone in our pursuits (1Pe. 5:9). It is very helpful to morale and to the vision as a whole that we take advantage of every opportunity to make people aware of what the Lord is doing in the Earth with regard to the establishment of His Global Prayer Movement.

Then Jesus told his disciples a parable to show them that they should always pray *and not give up… "will not God bring about justice for his chosen ones, who cry out to him day and night? Will he keep putting them off? I tell you, he will see that they get justice, and quickly. However, <u>when the Son of Man comes, will he find faith on the earth</u>?" (Luke 18:1, 7-8).*

- E. The Pursuit of Justice:
    1. Revival in our nation
    2. Ending of abortion
    3. Ending of sex trafficking

V. **Vision Casting Methods and Resources:**
- A. Events:
    1. National House of Prayer Leadership Summit
    2. TPR conferences
    3. Field trips to other houses of prayer

- B. Multimedia:
    1. Transformation Videos
    2. TPR Teaching Series
    3. TPR Prophetic History Series

- C. Books / Articles:
    1. *Charisma Magazine*, "The Church Braves Persecution in Indonesia"
    2. *The Heavenly Man* by Brother Yun and Paul Hattaway
    3. *Red Moon Rising* by Pete Grieg & Dave Roberts
    4. *Until He Comes* by Billy Humphrey

- D. Study Materials:
    1. Researching how HOPs are appearing all over the Earth
    2. The history of the prayer movement
    3. The bridal paradigm
    4. The end times

- E. Verbal Exhortations:
    1. Constant reminders of why this makes sense
    2. Bringing in other people to say the same thing you've been saying
    3. Testimonies from within your community about the power of prayer
    4. Short exhortations at the beginning of your prayer meetings

Session Eight: Growth Strategies

I. Brick by Brick:
My desire in this session is to share with you some of the building tools we have learned along the journey. I felt the Lord speak to me in our third year of doing daily prayer meetings that it was a season to "build the house of prayer brick upon brick" and that He would show me how. This session is comprised of many of the lessons and ideas that we felt the Lord give us in that time which proved to be very helpful building strategies.

II. Develop Recruiting Systems:
A. Promotional Media:
If no one knows that you are there, then no one will come. In our modern context, promotion is just as much a responsibility of the leadership as paying the bills. Some examples of promotion are listed below with the simple versions of each found in the parentheses.
1. Branding (logo, etc.)
2. Website
3. Facebook
4. Twitter
5. YouTube
6. E-flyers (email updates)

B. Physical Promotional Resources:
1. Business cards
2. Prayer schedules
3. Ministry pamphlets

C. Email Collection:
In order to send out email communication, you first have to have a database of email

addresses to send to. It is important to collect everyone's email address who visits your ministry. Create a simple sign in sheet for visitors so you can follow up later.

D. Personal Invitations:
Have people begin to actively hand these resources out around the city and to people they know. The concept of prayer meetings has not yet made the top priority list for much of the Church. By and large if they are going to come to your gatherings, it is going to be because someone asked them.

E. Follow Up:
You want to implement some method of following up with those who visit because most will not become an active part with just one visit to your ministry.

III. Begin Weekly Services:
This is essential to rally together and cast and keep vision. In addition to the obvious community dynamic that is added when you get everyone together in the same room, you will also find it necessary for the sake of making announcements and implementing changes and updates.

A. Fellowship:
It is invaluable to overall morale that relationships develop amongst those who are doing prayer meetings together. I highly recommend including a time of fellowship at your weekly gathering where they can enjoy some time together (perhaps over some snacks before or after your meeting).

B. Worship:
By gathering weekly in worship you will gain strength from that corporate time together in a way that is very different from the normal scattered few who participate in your daily prayer meetings. Corporate worship is a powerful unifying force. It helps to set us on a course together and remind us of who we are doing this for and that we don't journey it alone.

C. Teaching:
The teaching element of your weekly time together has a crucial role to play in that you will be focusing your teaching on subjects that are unique in two ways. First,

you will be teaching on themes that pertain to the thing you are all doing everyday (prayer, revival, intimacy and eschatology), and secondly these themes are mostly neglected in all the other teaching environments your community members frequent.

D. Vision Casting:

Without clearly identifying the purpose of what you are doing and the practical how you are going about doing it, your efforts won't make sense to people. It is important to regularly call the people to the vision and address them soberly to sign up to help build it. Your weekly meeting together - not email and not periodic events - is your primary platform to keep the vision before the community.

E. Offering Collection:

While I encourage you to keep your overhead as low as possible for as long as you can, you will doubtlessly have administrative costs. Take up an offering each week during your time of worship and give people the opportunity to partner with you financially. This will help provide for your monetary needs, but it also serves to get people connected at a deeper level to the vision and success of the ministry. Something happens in us when we sow our finances into a ministry; we begin to care at a new level.

IV. Introduce Ongoing Training:

With all the below ideas, the main purpose is to get people in the door who otherwise would not have come to your house of prayer or who come around but aren't really involved. The hope is that by their coming to one or more of the below trainings, they will catch more of the vision of your ministry, fall more in love with your community and so get involved in daily prayer meetings. Make sure that all of your training opportunities include a call to the vision at the front or back end of your meetings. Don't waste an opportunity to ask people to get involved in the main thing you do—prayer.

A. Prayer Leader Training:

Create a simple training for your prayer leaders. Have it include some biblical instruction about prayer and some direction about how you want people to pray and how not to be a distraction. Then make this training exclusive to those who are either leading prayer for you or who are interested in potentially becoming a prayer leader. You can develop multiple phases of this type of training so that even after someone has received the initial instruction, there are additional sessions that build on one another. You want to encourage people to attend these for several reasons, but first and foremost because you want them to get more involved. Specialized trainings such as this give people a sense of value and accomplishment, allowing them to feel like they have something to contribute.

B. Workshops:
Single night workshops are very helpful to get people to rally to. Even when we were small, we used to do one the last Sunday night of every month on a different subject. You may choose to bring in an outside speaker or you might have people in your community who can really do a great job for you. The key again is specialized trainings that people can't really get elsewhere; this is the draw for people.

C. Multi Session Training Series:
Plan specialized trainings on house of prayer related subjects that people are hungry for. Some examples of this may include: how to hear God's voice, introduction to the end times, how to build the house of prayer, etc. The purpose of these nights is to get people for a short-term commitment where they walk away with some depth on a subject that they couldn't have gotten in a single teaching.

D. Internships:
After you have gotten your feet wet by doing just a few of the above trainings, I advise you to consider launching an internship program. Your first internship can be as simple as a 5 hour a week commitment where interns sign up for two of your prayer meetings and attend a weekly internship instruction time that you develop. Have them also commit to helping with some small administrative task during the season of their internship (clean the bathroom, help make copies, etc.).

V. Invest in Community Building for Longevity:
As difficult as it is for people to commit to regular prayer meetings, you will need more than good organization to keep people around. It is essential that they bond together under the common vision and that they are afforded times just to enjoy each other. This section outlines the benefits of, and some strategies for, community building.

A. Benefits of the Community Dynamic:
1. Causes the people to enjoy each other
2. Builds overall morale when things are tough

Session 8: Growth Strategies

      3. Helps to sustain individuals
      4. Essential to the long-term sustainability of the ministry
      5. Happy people work harder

  B. **Encounter Service:**
      1. Time before or after your meetings
      2. Serve food before your weekly service
      3. Encourage people to go out together afterward

  C. **Community Building Events:**
      1. Potluck dinner at your facility
      2. Park day barbeque and games
      3. Planned dinner night at a restaurant
      4. Movie night (we've shown the transformation videos before)
      5. Seasonal activity

  D. **Specific Roles:**
  Assign people to specific roles within your organization chart so that they all share a part of the ministry together. This was covered in the session on "Building Your Team" but it has powerful effect on your ministry's community feel. As you grow a bit (even totaling at 15+ people), the people in the ministry who aren't part of your "staff" see the unique bond that is shared by those who are, and it creates a healthy longing for that measure of camaraderie.

VI. Weekly Think Tank Time:

Even the best of leaders run out of ideas and need to bring things back before the Lord and pray and strategize. For years I have regularly carved out an hour or two block of time just before the Lord in a time of prayerful brainstorming. This time is spent coming up with ideas that could help build the house of prayer and strengthen what we already have. I'll sit in front of my white board until it's full and then see what pieces may actually be helpful and then pray through whether (or when) to implement these ideas. This has always proven to be a good use of my time as the senior leader of this prayer ministry. We have been given charge to run our houses well, and excellence takes attention to details. These brainstorming times have continually kept more ideas before me than I have time to implement.

HOW TO BUILD A HOUSE OF PRAYER

A. **Improving Overall Excellence:**
There is always need to improve things in your ministry. Even if things were perfect 3 months ago, things have deteriorated since then and need tweaking and updating again.
1. What ways can you improve your communication?
2. How can you improve on your systems?
3. What documents need updating?

B. **Staff Growth and Changes:**
People like to feel "part" of the ministry. I advise getting as many people as possible involved in the running of your ministry as you can because the more people who take ownership of the vision, the more people you will have in prayer meetings and the more people you will have helping with the overall excellence of the ministry.
1. What new roles are you in need of?
2. What new people can you recruit to entry-level positions?
3. What existing people can you promote into more responsibility?
4. What staff holes can you create so you have holes to fill?

C. **Promotion and Retention:**
If we aren't constantly investing in getting new faces involved and working hard to love the ones who already are, then we will find ourselves in the difficult position of being undermanned.
1. How can you potentially get new faces in the door?
2. How can you help visitors connect with you better?
3. What can you do to connect with the community around you?

D. **Gathering Events:**
Events take a good bit of planning to pull off. But more than that, it takes a good bit of effort just to identify what sorts of events are the most helpful and productive for you.
1. What should be your next workshop?
2. Is there a teaching series that will draw people?
3. Are there any fun things you can do as a community?

E. **Next Steps:**
1. When can you add your next series of prayer meetings (remember we always add

Session 8: Growth Strategies

them across the board at the same time. Example: 7-9pm seven days a week)?

2. What ongoing program can you add next (Example: internship, weekly discussion groups, etc)?

3. When is the right time to get into a larger space?

VII. Creating Reasons for People to Get Involved:

No matter where you are as a prayer ministry, you want to invest some energy each season in implementing additional ways or reasons for people to become involved. As leaders we want to constantly have methods of recruiting new people to the Prayer Movement. There are many reasons people will get involved with your prayer ministry, and we want to implement as many of those reasons as we can carry in a healthy manner. By regularly strategizing about how to get more people more involved, you will constantly be taking your prayer ministry to the next step. Below are some common reasons why people get involved.

A. Prayer Related Reasons:
1. Some come because prayer is their thing
2. Some love justice issues
3. Some want to see revival

B. Relational Reasons:
1. Some come to be part of the community
2. Some will come around just because you're friendly
3. Some come because you gave them a way to serve

C. Like the Atmosphere:
1. Some come because of the worship music
2. Some just want a place to read their Bible

D. Encounter:
1. Some will come around because they feel God's presence
2. Some will find healing/deliverance
3. Some get involved because of the prophetic

E. Events:
1. Some will come for a conference
2. Some will come for a training
3. Some will come for a fun event

Session Nine: A Basic Prayer Model

I. Importance of a Prayer Model:

A prayer model helps guide your prayer meetings. It provides some simple guidelines about how the actual time during meetings should be spent. By implementing a model, you will immediately see a drastic difference in how quickly the time flies during your prayer meetings.

A. Organization:

Part of the reason behind why you want to have an established prayer model is the simple organizational side of things. There are many things that you are probably wanting to have happen, things you want people focused on and things that you really don't want people doing. Establishing a prayer model helps organize all this into some structure that you will find very helpful.

B. Setting Expectations:

A model helps everyone in the room know what to expect and what their boundary lines are, verses an everything-goes free-for-all. While those can sometimes be fun, they can also be disastrous to unity, and visitors don't have any idea what is going on.

C. Sustainability:

You have to approach the house of prayer differently than you do a once or twice a week prayer gathering. You have to build in such a manner that you can sustain it day after day, week after week, year after year. A prayer model is essential to long term sustainability.

II. Before You Even Create a Model:

A. Get Prayer Meetings Started:

Don't worry about a model until you actually have daily prayer meetings going. You can always improve on your new fledgling prayer ministry, but not until there is a ministry, which all the planning in the world cannot replace beginning it. Start meeting daily for prayer and then worry about a model.

B. The Sacred Trust:

Again the premise of The Scared Trust (call it whatever you want) is that individuals do more than a casual coming to prayer meetings, but that they call certain ones "Sacred" before the Lord. Individuals are encouraged to think and pray about their schedules and commit to one or more meetings per week that they will treat with an unusual respect, as holy. They would commit to attend these Sacred Trust prayer meetings at the cost of most everything else in their life, making the commitment to God that they will serve on the wall of intercession for that prayer meeting each week, and that God can count on them to serve Him faithfully in that place. This needs to be treated with sobriety. They aren't to designate all the prayer meetings as Sacred Trust, but only the ones that they will go way out of their way to attend. Our Sacred Trust permits a person to miss their committed prayer meetings only if they are very ill, have an unusual and unavoidable work conflict, a family emergency, are out of town or have a church conflict. In all other cases they are expected to attend what they themselves designate as Sacred. This means missing out on many opportunities, events, pleasures, etc. By implementing this structure, it becomes very reasonable to spread the responsibilities of the ministry because now you can ensure with just a little scheduling work that there is at least one person (hopefully a few) committed to each meeting.

C. You Have to Make the Commitment:

I strongly advise that the director/leader make the commitment to attend 100% of these prayer meetings to set the tone and to ensure the shift is covered. This ministry in its early days is far more about the work of the Lord in your own heart than even the building of night and day prayer. If the leader doesn't lead, then the people won't follow. Or if they do, they will quit and have disrespect for the leader because the leader, while casting the vision, isn't doing the work of daily prayer. I have been in morning prayer meetings seven days a week for over seven years now while having a full-time job (before being the full-time director), while having a wife and a kid, etc. It's doable; you just have to make it a priority.

Session 9: A Basic Prayer Model

III. Basic Meeting Requirements:

A. Where are You Going to Meet:

You need dedicated space. Identify a single location (the place and the room) where these daily prayer meetings will be happening. It needs to not rotate around so that you can easily communicate to people where you meet, as well as you won't have the added worry of schedule conflicts when one of your locations has something going on that requires the meeting to move. For 3 years we did 14 prayer meetings a week in my living room (one every morning and one every night). The living room was our dedicated space during those prayer times and nothing was allowed to take precedence over it. When I was going to be out of town or otherwise unable to be home, I put someone else in charge, but we kept prayer meetings going 7 days a week, 2 times a day for 3 years without fail. As a result, people really began to take us seriously.

B. When are Your Meetings:

Set the daily time that you will have prayer meetings (example: everyday from 6-7am or M-F from 8-9pm). Remember, that if your end goal is to have a House of Prayer that meets all the time, it is very reasonable that you would begin with daily meeting even in your early days as a ministry.

Schedule them according to what you the leader can most pull off in your schedule. You need to be in attendance at all or most of them if this is going to work, so pick a time that you can pull off in your daily schedule.

C. How Long will Your Meetings Last:

You never w ant your prayer meetings to become viewed as unimportant, so establish an amount of time that you commit to pray for and then never do less than that amount of time. If there is life on the meeting you can always go over, but never go under. If you say you meet for prayer each morning for an hour, then start praying on time and end on time not before. This will really help others to believe you are taking your prayer ministry seriously, as well as keep you from abbreviating meetings. If you start down that road it's far easier to excuse canceling a meeting all together because you normally meet for a shorter period of time on that day anyway.

D. Who will Attend:
1. Who will be on your "Sacred Trust"?
2. Are the meetings open to anyone?
3. Are you advertising or by invite only?

IV. Determining Themes and Formats:

A. Live Worship or MP3s:
Your model will look different depending on whether you will have live worship in your meetings or prerecorded worship such as CDs or MP3s playing throughout your set. With every prayer meeting that it is not possible to have a worship leader present, substitute with a worship CD. Develop this into your Prayer Model. In each set include times where intercession is the main focus with the music turned down but can still be heard, and then times of worship where the volume is turned up.

B. Format Types:
This is not an exhaustive list, but it should serve to help get you started in identifying the kinds of formats you want to utilize.

1. Devotional worship:

   These can be meetings where a worship leader leads for the entire time and the people in the room can sit and engage with the Lord by reading their Bible or quietly praying to themselves.

2. Corporate worship:

   These are times of worship where it is expected that everyone in the room engages the Lord together in song.

3. Intercession:

   Probably the type of prayer meeting that people are most used to calling "prayer." In this setting you build the prayer meeting around one of the topics listed under Themes, and you spend the bulk of the prayer meeting praying for various aspects of that overarching theme.

C. Choose Your Prayer Themes:
Each group has a different personality and each ministry a different calling, so you want to come up with themes and support topics that fit you. The purpose is to help the group more easily stay focused and unified in prayer.

1. Intercession themes:
   a. Ending of abortion
   b. God to raise up a prayer movement in the Earth
   c. God's plan for Israel
   d. For the Lord to visit your city in revival
   e. Anointing on various ministries
2. Worship themes:

Session 9: A Basic Prayer Model

   a. His majesty
   b. His beauty
   c. His justice

D. Sample Weekly Schedule:
1. Monday morning worship His beauty
2. Tuesday morning praying for the end of abortion
3. Wednesday morning praying for revival
4. Thursday morning praying for Israel
5. Friday morning worship His majesty
6. Saturday morning time of thanksgiving
7. Sunday morning worship His justice

V. Be Word Based:

People come from a variety of church backgrounds, and while we celebrate that diversity in the Body of Christ, it is important that in a corporate prayer meeting we are unified and in agreement. This requires that we have common ground that we all use as the basis of our prayers. The Bible is the written Word of God Himself and there is no better source of language and instruction about what God wants. We therefore have people pray the scriptures during our times of intercession. Anyone who wants to pray during these times can, but they must pray from the Word (the exception to this is during rapid fire discussed later). Below is a simple example script of what this looks like on a day when you are praying for the lost.

A. Identify:
"I'm going to be developing a prayer from Ephesians chapter 1 verse 17 asking the Lord to reveal Himself to the lost."

B. Read the Verse:
Ephesians 1:17 "I keep asking that the God of our Lord Jesus Christ, the glorious Father, may give you the Spirit of wisdom and revelation, so that you may know him better."

C. Pray It:
"Lord, allow the lost in our city to see You. Show them the falsehood of the world and the truth of who You are that they might know You."

VI. Define Team Roles:

As a means to strengthen both your community and your prayer meetings, it is a good idea to begin thinking about your model and ways to incorporate others into each meeting. Some examples of some of the roles that could be included are appointing a position for set up, one as an assistant prayer leader, a sound tech, etc. These roles are meant to add committed people to each shift and also to share the load for the responsibilities within a meeting. It is important for these roles to be a legitimate need and for people to understand the value of each role so they will take it seriously. By adding this simple step, you can double the amount of committed people to each meeting as they will, of course, be joining the Sacred Trust for whatever meeting they commit to serve in this capacity.

A. Prayer Leaders:

After some months of holding both regular prayer and regular teaching meetings, appoint a small number from among the faithful, to be Prayer Leaders. Begin having these individuals take on specific days or shifts as their own. This set actually accomplishes quite a bit; it begins the process of team building, allowing other members of the group to take some of the responsibility. It also releases some of the pressure from you so that you no longer have to lead all the meetings. It actually establishes your ministry to a far greater degree because there are now others taking a defined role in the success of the vision. You will find that by putting some of the weight into others hands they will have profound and helpful insights that will be a new source of inspiration.

B. Worship Leaders:

The Prayer Ministry is in many ways held together by its worship leaders. It will be very difficult to sustain prayer over the long haul without employing worship leaders in your meetings. At this point, you will really want to make a push for more worship leaders to join up with your cause. Begin by praying that God would send them to you and that He would soften those worship leaders around you to come and take part.

C. Musicians:

Set musicians or worship leaders in as many of the meetings as you can. It is a good idea to spread your potential worship leaders out over the course of your week so that you don't wear them out initially and so the meetings equally share this precious commodity (the worship leader). Throughout each meeting just have them be playing or strumming except for times of worship. You will find that by having live worship as a part of your meetings it will help the flow and enjoyability tremendously!

Session 9: A Basic Prayer Model

D. Assistant Prayer Leader:

This role is one of the great secrets to our success at The Prayer Room. We realized early on that we did not have any sort of abundance of singers, musicians and worship leaders, or for that matter attendance (most of our prayer meetings have had less than five people in them). We needed to try and figure out how to run as many intercession-like prayer meetings as we could, using just what we had. We developed the assistant prayer leader role as a way to be able to carry out a two-hour long prayer meeting with just three people; worship leader, prayer leader and assistant prayer leader. Obviously, the APL, as we refer to them, shares the load of prayer during the meeting along with the prayer leader, while the worship leader's sole responsibility is to lead worship during set times.

E. Usher:

We encourage you to get creative in creating additional roles that can be used to get people involved in your meetings. You may find that some people really want to avoid being upfront, in the spotlight so to speak, but that they genuinely want to have a part. We validate that and have them serve as an usher on that prayer team. Their main role is to connect with visitors when they come and to help them know what to expect in the prayer meetings as well as answer any questions they may have.

VII. Model Dynamics:

A. Worship:

Either with a CD or with live worship, be sure to implement times of worship into the meetings. This will aid you greatly in being able to sustain daily prayer meetings long term, as well as add dynamics to your meetings that make the time more enjoyable for those involved than if it was straight intercession for 60 minutes every day.

B. Antiphonal Singing:

Begin to introduce antiphonal singing (explained in our resource entitled "The Harp & Bowl Model") into your worship times. These are times where, after a season of introducing some of the Harp & Bowl Model dynamics, it may be time to reassess your prayer model and take it to the next step incorporating a more team approach to each meeting instead of just having a prayer leader and a worship leader.

C. Chorus Development:

At some point you will want to introduce the concept of creating new choruses in the middle of your prayer meetings so that people can engage together in united song about the thing you are praying about (also explained in the Harp & Bowl Model). We were able to do this even back in the living room days with no worship leader simply by appointing a chorus leader for that day. They would listen to the prayers begin prayed and then during a quiet moment (or even beginning quietly while someone else was still praying but then gaining volume as they finished) begin to develop a chorus about the thing that was just prayed, using even some of the same language from the previous prayer.

D. Spontaneous Singing:
The great part about spontaneous singing is that everyone does it together and so it really doesn't matter if no one can sing. The idea is to have everyone in the room begin out loud all at the same time to sing different things. One may be singing "Oh Lord I love you" while another may be singing "You've been so merciful to me all the days of my life." Have an appointed person (in most cases the worship leader) introduce a time of spontaneous singing during the meeting to get things started. We recommend using a key phrase like "lift your voices to the Lord" or "sing a new song to God" in your meetings so that you don't have to explain the concept every time.

E. Times of Intercession:
Of course build in times of focused intercession using the scripture as your guide and staple. These times of prayer are interspersed with the other model dynamics to create a more full canvas for your prayer meeting.

F. Rapid Fire:
This is a very helpful way to get everyone involved and also help with the lulls that often hit corporate prayer meetings. Rapid fire is intended to get everyone in the room to pray a quick 10-15 second prayer one after another in rapid succession (one at a time). Announce the rapid fire topic and then have everyone aim their short prayer at whatever that is. If you are in a prayer meeting praying for the lost to come to Christ, an example topic might be for people to pray for lost family members or friends to be saved.

VIII. Beginners Prayer Model (w/CDs):
A. Requirements:
1. One committed prayer leader
2. One hour long worship CD

Session 9: A Basic Prayer Model

    3. At least one other person in the room

B. Basic Time Chart (One Hour):
7:00-7:15 a.m. Worship (use a CD)
7:15-7:25 a.m. Intercession (sub topic 1)
7:25-7:30 a.m. One on one prayer for needs in the room
7:30-7:40 a.m. Intercession (sub topic 2)
7:40-7:50 a.m. Worship (use a CD)
7:50-8:00 a.m. Intercession (sub topic 3)

C. Recruit Worship Leaders:
Sit down with your group and make a list of every worship leader or musician that you can think of that someone in the group already has a relationship with. Ask God to give you some of the names on that list, for His Spirit to touch them in a special way where they would become inclined to your prayer ministry. Then in a few weeks implement some sort of plan for those who have previously established relationships with these different worship leaders to have a conversation with them about the Prayer Movement and the part your ministry is seeking to play.

IX. Basic Prayer Model with Live Worship:

A. Requirements:
1. Sound system and microphones
2. Committed prayer leader
3. Committed assistant prayer leader
4. Committed worship leader
5. Hopefully a couple of people in the room

B. Basic Time Chart (Two Hour):
6:00-6:30 p.m. Live Worship
6:30-6:50 p.m. Intercession (sub topic 1)
6:50-7:05 p.m. Live Worship
7:05-7:25 p.m. Intercession (sub topic 2)
7:25-7:40 p.m. Live Worship
7:40-8:00 p.m. Intercession (sub topic 3)

C. **Utilize the Model Dynamics:**
   As you begin to feel able, start implementing some of the various model dynamics discussed earlier in this session into your model. At this point you will probably also want to begin to start having debriefs after your prayer meetings to discuss ways to iron out some of the kinks in your model and communication.
   1. Antiphonal singing
   2. Chorus development
   3. Spontaneous singing
   4. Rapid fire

UNIT IV

Development

Session 10: Taking a Look at TPR's Departments

Session 11: Financing Your Work

Session Ten: Taking a Look at TPR's Departments

I. Department Heads:
Our ministry is divided into many different departments and then further into specific responsibilities that pertain to each department. We have department heads that serve as managers over the various responsibilities and support roles in that department. This session gives a basic overview of our organization and allows you to peer into how we utilize so many volunteers in running our full-time missions base.

II. Events Department:
A. Overall Reason Behind Events:
Calling people into the place of prayer is difficult. When talking to people about what we do at the house of prayer, we are mostly misunderstood, and the concept of living lives of prayer is mostly despised. Events, however, make sense to people in our culture. We use events to get people in the door so that we can hopefully have the opportunity to better explain what we are doing here and have a chance to make some sense to them by allowing them to see what we do first hand.

B. Encounter Services:
TPR's weekly Encounter Service is a time for the whole community to come together for a time of worship, fellowship and in depth Bible study where we focus on themes pertaining to prayer and the hour in which we live. Saturday nights are the one time each week that everyone from our various prayer meetings can all meet together, have vision cast for the House of Prayer, worship together, as well as fellowship and encourage one another. We invite anyone interested in who we are or what we are about to visit this weekly time where The Prayer Room gathers as one community.

C. Community Events:
From time to time members of the community plan game nights, pool parties, movie nights or community outings. Of course we are a people that love to eat, so groups sometimes just go out for a meal after an evening prayer meeting or donuts after an a.m. set. These events aren't planned, but fellowship and relationships are organic, so these impromptu outings form community as much as the structured events.

D. Conferences:
The Prayer Room hosts conferences on a variety of house of prayer related themes in order to inform, encourage and equip this generation into the Lord's purposes. We have hosted a number of conferences and brought in guest speakers on a few occasions to speak to and impassion our community.

E. Workshops:
The Prayer Room offers workshops several times a year to help the local church understand the fundamentals and reality of prayer. We rotate our workshop topics to cover a broad range of subjects including: praying the Apostolic prayers, harp and bowl worship, growing in the prophetic, marketplace Christianity, cultivating a life of prayer and more.

III. Staffing Department:

A. Importance of Having Staff:
1. Provides a workforce
2. Keeps The Prayer Room going

B. Various Roles & Functions:
1. Individualized roles
2. Splits up the responsibilities

C. Volunteer Staff:
1. Creates easy on ramps for people to increase involvement
2. Only requires one or two hours of admin per week

D. Intercessory Missionaries:
1. Internship required
2. Part-time positions (easier on ramp for those who feel called)

Session 10: Taking a Look at TPR's Departments

      3. Full-time positions (higher financial support minimum)

  E. Staff Funding:
      1. Raising support
      2. Create a giving culture in your community
      3. Always look for ways to help them
      4. Reduced housing
      5. Small stipends / periodic bonuses

IV. Prayer Room Operations:

  A. Running our Prayer Room:
    It takes many specific roles all laboring together in order to keep our prayer room running each week. Prayer room operations is broken down into various categories and sub departments that have unique responsibilities. Everyone works together to pull off the running of this prayer furnace.

  B. Prayer Room Etiquette and Procedures:
    It is our desire to present to the Lord a meeting place where saints can come at any time and engage in prayer and worship. In order to create this environment, it is necessary that we all follow some basic standards for the common enjoyment of the prayer room.
      1. Talking policy:
         Keep conversations under 30 seconds, and please speak quietly. When praying personally, please aim not to be a distraction to those around you.
      2. Food & drink:
         There is no eating allowed in the prayer room at any time. All beverages must be in a spill proof bottle (this means you must be able to turn your beverage upside down without any spilling).
      3. Phone use:
         Please do not make or take any phone calls while you are in the prayer room.
      4. Personal worship instruments:
         Please do not use any personal worship instruments at any time (shofars, tambourines, etc.). If you are interested in trying out for a team, please contact our worship department.
      5. Do not disturb:
         It is our desire to maintain an environment where anyone, whether TPR staff,

local pastors, or anyone from the surrounding community can come pray, read, or work undisturbed. For this reason please do not approach or disturb others who are engaging in prayer, worship, or work (please wait until they leave the prayer room).

6. Sleeping:
Sleeping is not permitted during your Sacred Trust prayer meetings. (If it's not your Sacred Trust, please come take a nap.)

7. Pets policy:
We ask that you do not bring your pets into the prayer room; this place of prayer was created for people, not animals. Licensed service animals are an exception.

8. Clean up after yourself:
Whatever you may have brought in with you, please be sure to remove when you leave. Also straighten up any chairs or anything else you may see out of place.

C. Section Leaders:

The vision that we have for our section leaders is that they would manage their block of time well, working out whatever holes and problem solving whatever may come up. They need to be able to take responsibility for whatever shift they are over and to find someone (person or persons must be approved by Directors first) to take their place in all of their responsibilities if an absence is required. We want for our Section Leaders to take complete responsibility for what happens during their shift and be able to give account for anything related, even in the case that certain tasks have been assigned out to others. We want our Section Leaders to think of themselves as the director on duty for their 4 hour block, handling any problems, absences, delinquencies, follow ups, inconsistencies or the like, doing their best to correct any issues that arise.

D. Worship Teams:

1. Team dynamic:
Each set has its own worship team. Some teams are as small as just one person, the worship leader, and other sets are full with singers, musicians and prayer leaders, etc. The team dynamic is very important to our overall philosophy of ministry, going far beyond our prayer model. Every person on the team has a different role and specific responsibilities to perform that cause the symphony to come together.

2. Team captain:
The worship leader is the captain of the team, and he or she leads the worship set. They also help form what that team looks like and can recruit people to join them

Session 10: Taking a Look at TPR's Departments

   in the various positions.
3. Continual need:
   We are constantly looking for singers and musicians to get involved. As we build toward 24/7 prayer, we endeavor to continually add new prayer shifts, which requires building additional worship teams. Our model utilizes a variety of roles and skill sets in each prayer meeting. Currently we are auditioning singers and musicians and need prayer leaders and assistant prayer leaders as well. Our greatest need is for those who would be able to help us establish strong worship teams by joining one or more sets per week.

E. The Sacred Trust:
The Sacred Trust is a documented prayer schedule that contains a list of each individual's commitment to specific prayer meetings. It is given this name because we want to keep our commitment (Trust) with all diligence, as something that is sacred or holy before the Lord. The way we do this is by placing supreme value in our attendance and attitude towards the Lord's call for night and day prayer.
1. Even when it hurts:
   Although we may not always have desire for prayer burning in our hearts, we maintain that the prayer meetings we have committed to are very important to the Lord. We therefore choose to turn down many other activities in order to hold to our commitment to be at our prayer meetings and to be on time. This is not always easy, but if we maintain a vision for its value and treat the Sacred Trust accordingly, we can hold our hearts steadfastly and respond rightly to Jesus' invitation in Luke 18.
2. Practically sustaining prayer:
   Apart from the Sacred Trust, we cannot realistically expect that sustained 24/7 prayer will exist. If, however, everyone shares the load and commits to various prayer shifts, we can build night and day prayer in DFW. It takes people in order to have prayer meetings.
3. A tool for your prayer life:
   The Sacred Trust exists to help you make sure a set time of prayer every week is kept holy before the Lord. The Prayer Room welcomes everyone to join our community and will encourage them in any way we can.

V. Base Operations:
A. Janitorial:

HOW TO BUILD A HOUSE OF PRAYER

The janitorial role tends to all of the cleaning needs of our missions base, both for regular weekly operations as well as whatever special requirements come up from time to time.

B. Ordering of Supplies:
The missions base has dozens of items that we need ordered each month. If someone isn't specifically assigned to this responsibility, then we run out of needed supplies.

C. Maintenance:
Light bulbs need to be replaced, wiring needs to be fixed, new things need to be hung and old things need to be fixed. We have someone over maintenance to make sure that all these things get taken care of.

D. Set Up:
Each week there are things that require setting up and rearranging. The person over set up sees to it that our base is in good order for the normal flow of our operations, as well as taking care of set up and tear down for special events.

E. Construction:
Whenever we do a building project of any sort, make an addition at our base, or move from one facility to another, we need a point person to oversee and manage that project.

VI. Finance Department:
Without finances the ministry would not be able to function. Having an organized finance department is essential to the operations of a missions base. We have a simple but effective manner or organizing things.

A. Accounts Receivable:
Accounts receivable is responsible to keep track of the funds we have coming in. They are responsible to count the donations weekly, monitor our online giving and then update our spreadsheets that keep track of the income. They follow up with those who have made pledges to our intercessory missionaries or as a TPR Partner and handle any questions our staff might have. They also ensure that our Saturday night offering runs smoothly.

Session 10: Taking a Look at TPR's Departments

B. Accounts Payable:
Accounts Payable writes the checks, makes deposits and pays the bills. Then they record all the expenses into our financial program each month and reconcile any late bills or expenses. They coordinate with departments on policies regarding monthly purchases and in many cases make the purchases on behalf of the various departments.

C. Business Revenue:
In order to operate, we reply on several forms of revenue, not donations solely. All finances that we receive because of the sale of a product, service or event we keep track of separately. This helps us to know if the programs we are offering are hopefully at least breaking even.
1. Sale of books or other resources
2. Registration for conferences and one day seminars
3. Payment for a community ministry trip

VII. Forerunner Equipping Center:
Because I will spend a good bit of time developing our FEC in the session entitled "Expanding Once You're Established," I will only give a brief overview here and focus on the aspects that make us distinct.

A. Overall Reason Behind FEC:
At The Prayer Room we want to try and find the best ways to provide effective training that also provides for the financial needs of the ministry.

B. Internships:
Our Internship is a part-time commitment of 20+ hours per week. Both the 16-week Spring and Fall Semester or the 8-week Summer intensive offers interns the opportunity to be fully immersed into the vision and values of the House of Prayer. During this season of consecration, interns will be challenged greatly in their walk with the Lord. Interns will be taught how to go deep in prayer, having both their Bibles and the person of Jesus opened up to them in a very new way. We focus on training and equipping our interns in a lifestyle of prayer. This also provides the opportunity to see firsthand how to run a missions base. Upon graduation, interns are given the option as well as instructions on how to join part or full time staff with The Prayer Room

C. Music Academy:

TPR's Forerunner Music Academy is a part time training school (approximately 10 hours per week) aimed at worship leaders, singers and musicians. From the beginner musician to the advanced worship leader, FMA exists for all those wanting to cultivate a passionate heart of worship and lead others into deeper encounter with His Spirit through anointed music. No matter what venue you lead, play or sing in, this school will cause your heart to grow deeper in love Christ, to increase in your skill level and excellence on the platform as well as equip you with the tools you need to help others connect with the Lord's heart in Worship.

D. School of Ministry:

The Forerunner School of Ministry is a part time Bible School that is semester based, offering tracks that build on one another. We offer select courses from our curriculum each semester that are open to all and available for sign up on a course-by-course basis, or a student may choose to participate in all of the courses offered that semester.

E. School of the Prophetic:

The School of the Prophetic lays the foundation for the lifestyle that is required to grow in hearing the voice of the Lord. The course focuses on practical application and is applicable to individuals varying in all levels of prophetic experience. Students will gain a great Biblical foundation of the role and use of prophecy and can expect to grow greatly in their confidence of hearing and giving prophetic words. Experienced students will learn how to fine-tune their ear and lifestyle to go to the next level in prophetic and personal ministry. During this course our students will be immersed in the place of prayer, will learn to give and receive prophetic words and be greatly encouraged in their faith.

VIII. Promotions Department:

A. Importance of Promotions:

Until your ministry is in full-on revival, promoting your ministry is such an important aspect of what you do. There are many people who would want to become involved in the house of prayer but they don't have the information they need; perhaps they don't even know you exist.

Session 10: Taking a Look at TPR's Departments

B. **Having a Web Presence:**
Any ministry that doesn't have a website is sending a message to this generation not to take them seriously. It's fine if you don't have a phone number, but you have to have a website these days for people to find you and see what you are about.

C. **Facebook Campaigns:**
1. Reach most people:
   Again, you need some sort of Facebook presence to reach the broadest number of people.
2. Check-in:
   People can Check-In on their mobile devices. This shows up on their timeline for all their friends to see. That's great free publicity.
3. Invites:
   Create invites for all special events and then enlist your community's help.

D. **E-flyers:**
It's important to find the balance between how many eflyers is too much and how many is not enough. Too many email e-flyers will result in recipients not reading your communication and/or requesting to be removed from your mailing list. Not enough e-flyers will result in your mailing list recipients missing important updates/events. You also want to send out enough communication so that they never forget your ministry is out there.

E. **Concerted Efforts:**
1. Focus:
   It's important that all email communications are intentional and focused (versus a shotgun approach). This approach is far more effective. Look at all the upcoming events/needs/communication and then decide which one or two are most important and then highlight these in your communications.
2. Too much:
   A shotgun approach would be sending out communication with the top 10 things happening at the ministry in the coming weeks. This is overwhelming for the recipient, and they're likely to not read all (or any) of the communication.
3. Announcements:
   Announcements during corporate meetings are good times to share more than the one or two premiere events that you have upcoming but be intentional even about this time so that the community doesn't get overwhelmed and/or tune out.

HOW TO BUILD A HOUSE OF PRAYER

F. Branding:
1. Credibility:
   Branding is important so that people recognize your ministry; it lends credibility and provides continuity.
2. Use your logo:
   At TPR we have the logo that is placed on all our communications – emails, print materials, signs, etc.
3. Streamlining:
   We also have themes that provide continuity within the ministry. For example, all the Forerunner Equipping Center programs have similar graphics to easily identify them as FEC programs.

G. Google Analytics:
1. General web tracking:
   TPR's website has a feature that tracks how many hits each page gets in a given time frame. Many template-based websites will have a similar feature.
2. Using Google Analytics:
   Google Analytics is a free program that is infinitely more powerful which allows you to see which pages on your website are viewed most often. This information will allow you to decide which pages are most important to viewers so you can edit your website accordingly.

H. Graphics & Video:
Simplicity is the key. In our early days we designed graphics as simply and professionally as possible without spending any money and without anyone with specific graphic skills on staff. Now TPR has a graphic artist on our staff, which is a great asset for us.

Session Eleven: Financing Your Work

I. Importance of Finances:

Not long after you begin, you will be faced with an endless list of things that you wish you had, all of which would help improve the ministry and all of which cost money. The longer you go, the longer that list gets and the more expensive the items on that list become. I can remember when we started prayer meetings in my living room, the most expensive thing we needed was for some copies to be made or for something to be laminated. 7 years later I'm trying to figure out how to buy buildings and pay salaries.

II. Getting a Vision for God's Partnership:

A. Importance of the Extravagant Giving:

We really want to be able to develop faith for finances. The best way to do that is to build a history with God in our giving, not just us as individuals but as a ministry. We want a rich history of sowing into the things that make His heart glad. My suggestion is that as a ministry you give away at least 10% of what you bring in with a goal of giving more than that.

> *"Give, and it will be given to you. A good measure, pressed down, shaken together and running over, will be poured into your lap. For with the measure you use, it will be measured to you" (Luke 6:38).*

> *Remember this: Whoever sows sparingly will also reap sparingly, and whoever sows generously will also reap generously. Each man should give what he has decided in his heart to give, not reluctantly or under compulsion, for God loves a cheerful giver. And God is able to make all grace abound to you, so that in all things at all times, having all that you need, you will abound in every good work (2 Corinthians 9:6-8).*

B. David's 100 Billion Dollar Gift to the Prayer Movement:

God really wants His House built. David in his day was able to give over 100 billion dollars to build the House of Prayer. Who knows what that would be equal to in modern terms?! God isn't limited; we need to keep that in mind.

> *"With all my resources I have provided for the temple of my God—gold for the gold work, silver for the silver, bronze for the bronze, iron for the iron and wood for the wood, as well as onyx for the settings, turquoise, stones of various colors, and all kinds of fine stone and marble—all of these in large quantities. Besides, in my devotion to the temple of my God I now give my personal treasures of gold and silver for the temple of my God, over and above everything I have provided for this holy temple: three thousand talents of gold (gold of Ophir) and seven thousand talents of refined silver, for the overlaying of the walls of the buildings, for the gold work and the silver work, and for all the work to be done by the craftsmen"*
> *(1Chronicles 29:2-5).*

C. End Time Redistribution of Wealth:
There is promise of a great shifting of wealth in the Last Days into the hands of the Prayer Movement so that God's powerful purposes might be released.

> *This is what the LORD Almighty says: "<u>In a little while</u> I will once more shake the heavens and the earth…and I will fill this house with glory,' says the LORD Almighty. 'The silver is mine and the gold is mine,' declares the LORD Almighty. '<u>The glory of this present house will be greater than the glory of the former house</u>,'"*
> *says the LORD Almighty (Hg. 2:6-9).*

III. Identifying Your Financial Inroads:

This section is essential for the para-church expressions, while everyone, no matter what type of ministry we lead, can glean ideas.

A. Tithes and Offerings:
1. For the para-church expressions:
   a. Surrounding churches:
   As a para-church ministry it is extremely important that we develop good relationships with the surrounding local churches. After all, every one of the people who comes to pray in your meetings attends church somewhere, and it would be good to stay on good terms with their pastors wherever possible.
   b. Unavoidable conflict:
   Sometimes conflict will be unavoidable because a leader just doesn't like what you stand for or something else that is out of your control.
   c. Avoidable conflicts:
   But you want to do all that you can to support the local pastors around you, espe-

cially with regard to money. You will find it difficult to gain respect in your city if the people who are coming around your ministry are tithing to you instead of to their local church. My advice is that you do what you can to discourage that.
   d. Over and above:
   Now that you've discouraged tithing, you want to encourage over and above giving, or the giving of offerings. Admittedly this scenario is one of the most difficult situations to navigate, and it is one of the main drawbacks of all para-church expressions.
2. For the local church expressions:
   You want to continue to put your best foot forward with your church leadership, showing them the results of your efforts. You want them to know about answered prayers, about transformed lives and about your future plans. This type of communication is the best way to keep your department (the House of Prayer) funded.

B. Community Pledges:
1. Asking specific people:
   At a bare minimum you want to ask those who are committed to the ministry to make a monthly financial commitment at whatever amount they can afford.
2. Staff participation:
   We have all of our staff make monthly financial commitments to the ministry in whatever amount they decide. The point here is just to make sure that the people who are most involved have some skin in the game and some vested interest in our success.
3. Community involvement:
   Make it known to the larger community that your ministry is attempting to raise a budget and that monthly pledges are of the greatest need.

C. Praying for the Finances:
Let us not forget who our supplier is and how it is that finances are ultimately released. As leaders we need to develop regular habits of asking the Lord to release the finances to us that we need and that we desire to use to build the work He gave us to oversee. Let us not be guilty of not asking.

> *"Ask and it will be given to you; seek and you will find; knock and the door will be opened to you. For everyone who asks receives; he who seeks finds; and to him who knocks, the door will be opened…If you…know how to give good gifts to your children, how much more will your Father in heaven give good gifts to those who ask him!" (Matthew 7:7-11).*

HOW TO BUILD A HOUSE OF PRAYER

> *You do not have, because you do not ask God. When you ask, you do not receive, because you ask with wrong motives, that you may spend what you get on your pleasures (James 4:2-3).*

IV. Business Model Income:

A. Developing Business Relations:

1. Joseph Company:
   Something that IHOP has wisely done was to launch a ministry under their umbrella that focuses on calling and equipping people in the workforce to financially partner with the House of Prayer. They call this ministry the Joseph Company, pointing to the position that Jacob's son, Joseph, acquired in Egypt that allowed him to use the wealth of the wicked to financially prosper the people (Kingdom) of God.

2. Building relationships with local businessmen:
   We want to both build new relationships and strengthen the relationships that we already may have in our midst. One of the best ways to do this is to make a point to pray with and for those who are in positions of leadership in their work or who have the capacity in their line of work for wealth. We do not discount praying for the guys in our midst who make minimum wage working at the coffee shop; we just approach him differently as his current scenario probably doesn't include an active calling to fund the House of Prayer.

3. Marketplace prayer meetings:
   a. Praying for individuals in the marketplace by name
   b. Praying for those in your midst who need jobs, or better jobs
   c. Praying for divine ideas to hit members of the community
   d. Praying for the protection of jobs for the community
   e. Praying for the increase of salaries and for bonuses

B. Church Partners:

Depending on your circumstances, you may be in the place to approach other ministry leaders about helping to financially partner with your ministry. As a para-church ministry this is especially valuable because it can forge some good relational lines between you and a nearby congregation. You commit to pray for the needs of that church and that local church commits to help fund your work. Often churches have a missions budget that they regularly reassess and determine what ministries they will be investing in.

Session 11: Financing Your Work

C. Sale of Resources:
As soon as you are able, begin producing your own resources from your teaching and training times. These can yield your ministry an additional source of income.

D. Paid Programs:
A major source of income for most all of the successful Houses of Prayer (of all sizes) is their use of short-term training schools and internships. We recommend developing something simple and starting small, you can always expand as you grow. Even a small fee of $100 for a simple three-month internship can bring revenue into your ministry's budget.

V. Intercessory Missionaries Raising their Own Salary:
By having all of your staff raise their own missionary support, you are able to keep your overhead significantly lower. This makes a huge difference in your overall finances and permits you to begin "hiring" paid staff much earlier than if you had to raise their salaries through the ministry.

A. Intercessory Missionaries in the Word:
1. David's 4000 gatekeepers (1Ch. 23:5)
2. David's 4000 singer/musicians (1Ch. 23:5)
3. Nehemiah's priests and singers (Ne. 13:10-122)
4. Anna (Lk. 2:36-37)

B. Role of the Extended Internship:
Before we have someone commit to raising support and serving as a paid staff member, we will want for them to have gone through a fairly intense internship with us first. A typical internship should last at least a couple months and include all of the aspects of what would be expected as a full time staff person, though perhaps in lesser degree. For instance, our part time internship is a pre-requisite to coming on staff and it requires 5 prayer meetings per week, joining a fasting team at whatever level they wish to participate, attending our Encounter Service, having a weekly service responsibility as well as attending 7-10 hours of class each week. All in all, this puts them up at the base for around 25 hours each week.

1. Internships provide frame of reference:
   If someone is going to raise support, and they have not been immersed in the lifestyle of the House of Prayer first, the individual may get a bunch of supporters

and raise his/her funds and then 1 month in decide that it's too hard or not what they expected and just quit. This reflects very poorly upon your ministry and will make it more difficult for future missionaries to raise their support.

2. Internships test character:
If a missionary's character has not been properly investigated, you may be very sorry that you are permitting them to represent your ministry and even find yourself in a place where you have to remove them from staff. A 3 or 4 month long internship gives you reasonable time to identify what manner of person they are and to decide whether you want them on your paid staff.

3. Internships impart vision:
It is crucial that missionaries are given a season of understanding the why behind the what that internships are geared toward imparting. Once someone decides to come on staff, all of the Enemy's ploys are launched against that individual. If they are not rooted in what the Bible has to say about what they are doing, they will quickly lose heart and vision for it.

C. Support Raising Process:
Once an individual has gone through your internship and passed all your requirements, then it comes time to raise support. This is a major hurdle that each missionary has to overcome. We have an entire support raising course that we offer, as well as tools that may help your staff in their support raising process. Below are some of the things our staff utilizes.

1. Support raising binder
2. One on one visits
3. Video ask
4. Personalized email process
5. Hand written notes
6. Crucial nature of follow-up
7. Blog or e-newsletters
8. We offer a support raising course that we recommend

UNIT V

Starting to Build

Session 12: Administrative Steps

Session 13: From the Ground Up

Session 14: Expanding Once You're Established

Session Twelve: Administrative Steps

I. Introduction:

The purpose of this session is to identify the practical administrative steps that you will need to take in order to establish your prayer ministry. Most of the steps included here are not unique to the house of prayer but would be helpful for getting any ministry started. It's been my experience that many of those who the Lord is calling to build His house are pioneers who have never had to form a ministry before and don't have anywhere to identify the proper steps to take. When we started off, I certainly had zero experience to these simple steps; not even enough exposure to them to know that these were things I was supposed to do. Now that we've been helping ministries launch for some years, we've found the details of this session to be invaluable for many.

II. Forming Your Website and Social Media:

We live in a generation that is increasingly more multimedia driven and where social networking is no longer only about connecting with friends but is now greatly about marketing and branding as well. If we are going to try and reach a generation of 20-year-olds, we will have to appeal to them. The issue isn't that people won't stay around if we don't have cool graphics, it's that there will be such a large section of our target audience that we will never have been given the opportunity to get through our doors because we didn't do a good job presenting and introducing our ministry via the primary avenue that 20-year-olds access: internet and social media.

A. Three Categories of People:
1. Not a chance:
   There are many of those out there who won't come get involved with your ministry no matter what you do or how you package things.
2. Absolutely:
   Then thankfully there are a few of those who you won't be able to stop from

getting involved with you pretty much no matter what you do because they are divinely hijacked by the Lord on your behalf.

3. Maybe:

The third category, however, is the larger majority that we can't afford to neglect. I don't in any way think that marketing strategies or social media is our savior and the only means by which people decide whether to come get involved in a ministry or not. But these factors certainly do play a role in the discussion, and there are many who really would have come and gotten involved if a more concentrated effort of letting them know about your ministry had been made. This is the audience we are trying to capture.

B. Logo Development:

As a first step that will serve to unify your ministry and help to identify who you are to others, you want to develop your own logo. Most everyone takes the approach of reinventing some sort of flame for their logo, which in one sense has become a brand for the prayer movement. We recommend, however, that you change up more than just the flame to form your logo but also to modify the concept and create something unique that identifies your ministry. You can always pay a graphics artist to help you with this process.

C. Creating Graphics:

Keeping in mind that your primary audience, at least for most ministries, is the 20-year-old crowd, presentation matters. This generation learns far more by sight and interaction than by wordy explanations. To draw in your target audience, you need to communicate to them in ways they relate to. I am in no way referring to using the wicked marketing schemes that the lost world around us uses, but I do mean having graphics that depict what you are trying to present.

1. Identify who can help you:

   You may have to hire from without for your graphics until the Lord sends you someone; we did this for a number of years.

2. Concept matching:

   General graphics that don't relate to your subject matter are distracting rather than helpful. It is important that whatever you display visually helps to develop the concept(s) that you are actually presenting.

3. Graphic to text ratios:

   There may not be any set ratios that have to be followed regarding text to image percentages, but it is important to say as much as is necessary to convey the concept in as few words as possible. Many make the mistake of presenting too much information in paragraph after paragraph with perhaps a header graphic (or none at all) at the top. This is a sure way to lose a large portion of your target audience who are used to concise and clever.

D. Website:
1. Relevance:
   In this day and age, in order to be considered legitimate, a web presence is essential.
2. Finding what you need:
   A few years ago we made a change and started using a template based website that has proven to be perfect for our needs. Our needs, much like most of yours, is that we needed something that we could change ourselves whenever we needed to make updates but something that was simple enough that someone with little, if any, technical skills could figure out.
3. Recommendation:
   Normally the template based web hosts provide a very cookie cutter looking product and your website ends up being bland and boxy, but we found one that I would like to recommend to you called Radiant Webtools (found at www.radiantwebtools.com) which has proven to have a ton of flexibility and can be made to look very professional without having to know html (website programming language). Our current site costs us about $70/month but there are far cheaper options as low as $25 a month.

E. E-flyers and Contact Management:
1. Growing your contacts:
   Another extremely important tool to have in operation is some sort of way to manage your growing database of contacts. You want to be keeping track of those who visit your ministry, getting at least their email address so that you can continually increase your reach.
2. Management program:
   At the very least keep track of these in an Excel spreadsheet, but we would recommend paying for a monthly service that offers a way to keep track of your contacts online that also offers the ability to create and send eflyers to your growing contact base.
3. E-flyer program:
   There are many programs out there that offer the combined service of contact

management and eflyer creation/sending. We use a service called Constant Contact (found at www.constantcontact.com) that helps you to easily make professional looking eflyers that can be sent as often as you like to whatever groups of your contacts make sense for a particular communication.

F. Getting into Social Media:

You want to take advantage of as much free promotion as you can get your hands on. The more that your ministry and logo is out there on the web and via social media, the better chance there is that people will take notice of you. Further, there is a compounding effect that occurs in brand recognition. The more times and the more avenues that someone sees your brand, the more likely they are to remember you or pay attention. We live in an hour where people's attention is constantly being fought for and, the amount of images and information that the average person takes in a day is astounding; low estimates put that number in the hundreds. What if it's been two weeks since your brand has been in front of an individual who was really thinking about coming to get involved? There is a real chance that they will forget, be distracted, etc. All of the below have their place in the discussion of establishing and maintaining your branding, and you would do well to invest some energy as your ministry grows.

1. Facebook
2. YouTube
3. Twitter
4. Mass text service
5. Others besides

III. Setting Up Your Ministry

A. Consult a CPA:

Unless you have a good handle on non-profit tax laws we recommend paying a CPA to help you form your ministry so that things are handled in an efficient and legal manner. This will especially be important later down the road as your ministry grows and you will be glad that you established things in a right order. The costs for such services can vary, but it is reasonable to get everything done for about $1000.

B. File with the State:

If you are utilizing a CPA, they will do this for you. What is important for you to know is that as far as the state is concerned you are a business first and foremost,

Session 12: Administrative Steps

so you have to follow the process of filing as a corporation (there are several designations) before you are able to become a tax-exempt corporation (aka a non-profit ministry).

C. File 501(c)3 for Non-Profits:
The form that you use to become a non-profit ministry is Form 501(c)3, which is commonly referenced in the ministry world simply as 501(c)3. Once you have been approved, this allows your ministry to offer tax exemption on donations given to your ministry; this can be an added incentive for people to give.

D. Create a Simple Budget:
Even when we were back in my living room, we had a working budget that identified our monthly expenses and desired expansions (instruments, new endeavors, promotions, etc.). Spend some time creating a proposed monthly budget and then present the needs to the people involved in your ministry to see if they may be able to help. It is important that you establish good spending habits while you are still small.

IV. Getting Your Director Full Time:

A. Assessing Your Future:
While no one really knows what the future holds for their ministry, we all do our best to try and lead according to what we are sensing is the Lord's direction. If you feel that the final intention for your house of prayer is to have just a few hours of prayer each day and you don't have any intention of trying to grow into something bigger, then there is a lot about this handbook that doesn't need to apply to you. If, however, you feel that the Lord is leading you to build some version of night and day prayer, offer training and eventually have paid staff, then you will need a full-time director eventually.

B. Importance of a Full Time Leader:
It takes a tremendous amount of effort to keep something running 6 or more hours a day 7 days a week. With programs and events on top of that, we're talking 50 hours a week minimum. It requires a full-time leader at the helm to establish systems, to be there just to make sure things are running smoothly and to do all the additional administrative efforts that keep a ministry running. Most churches aren't open near that much per week, and yet we see the wisdom of paying a senior pastor a salary and having them pastor as their full-time occupation.

HOW TO BUILD A HOUSE OF PRAYER

C. Immediate Increased Productivity:
As soon as you are able to get yourself fulltime, I recommend that you do so because your concentrated efforts as the visionary will help things to grow much quicker with you full time. This of course will benefit every aspect of the ministry and everyone involved, because a more organized ministry is a better ministry and a director who is free to be in lots of prayer meetings is a better leader.

D. Support Raising Process:
1. Concept of the intercessory missionary:
   There was a time in America where the concept of giving someone money so that they could go to another country and tell people about Jesus was new, nonsensical and even offensive to some. We now refer to this concept as foreign missions and it is widely accepted in most of the Church as valuable. Many of these same hang-ups exist now regarding the concept of funding someone to pray all day, a term we call intercessory missionary.
2. Biblical foundation:
   But this concept is well founded in the Word of God from the time of Moses onward. In fact, when Nehemiah heard that the intercessory missionaries of his day weren't receiving their finances, he was furious and demanded that the money be given them so that they wouldn't have to work other jobs but could give themselves to the fulltime work of prayer and worship.

   I also learned that the portions assigned to the Levites had not been given to them, and that all the Levites and singers responsible for the service had gone back to their own fields. So I rebuked the officials and asked them, "Why is the house of God neglected?" Then I called them together and stationed them at their posts. All Judah brought the tithes of grain, new wine and oil into the storerooms. I put Shelemiah the priest, Zadok the scribe, and a Levite named Pedaiah in charge of the storerooms (Nehemiah 13:10-13).

3. Financial reasoning for support raising missionaries:
   Plain and simple, it takes a lot of money to pay someone a salary, and much more to pay two people for full time work. But the house of prayer isn't mostly looking at having two staff members. In fact those who are doing it well estimate that it takes 200 or more to maintain 24/7 with live worship in a sustainable way. Where in the world is any ministry going to find sufficient funding to pay 200 staff salaries? But if the staff all raises their own missionary support and then we do everything within our power to help them, hopefully by being able to help provide inexpensive housing, many even small stipends as we grow, then there is potential-

Session 12: Administrative Steps

ly no limit to how many staff a house of prayer might have.

4. You must lead the way:

   If your ministry set up can afford to help you by providing a stipend that will be of great help to get you started. But you as the director need to raise your own support as a missionary at least for a few years so that you know the difficulties of what you are asking your staff to do. This will cause them to respect you far greater than if you don't or have never had to go through the rigors of the experience. These funds need to be raised personally from your own sphere of influence and contacts, and these funds are in addition to the general ministry budget. If you as the leader can't raise support, it is unrealistic to ask others to. Instead you need to pave the way. This will help you to minister to the countless others who follow in your footsteps.

V. Creating Staff Roles and Descriptions:

A. Define Standard Staff Commitments:

I knew that our staff was going to be mostly comprised of people giving of themselves in a very limited way; that they had full time jobs and families and other responsibilities besides. When we started to form our "volunteer staff" I kept all that in mind, but it had to be balanced with the fact that we were going to be calling these people "staff." So we came up with what has proven to be a challenging but very doable set of standard commitments that every member of our staff upholds. Here is a simplified list of those commitments.

1. Weekly commitment to two Sacred Trust prayer meetings
2. Commitment to serve on those meetings in some assigned role
3. Weekly attendance at the Saturday night Encounter Service
4. Attendance at our weekly hour-long staff meeting
5. Participation in weekly fasting by joining a fasting team
6. Commitment to be actively involved at their local church
7. Serve in some small administrative role within our organization

B. Begin Enlisting Staff Members:

I want to encourage you to begin the volunteer staff concept immediately and begin enlisting people. If I could go back, I would have started this much sooner, I just hadn't thought of it yet. Once you put this into place, you will see an increase in several areas of your ministry.

1. More buy-in and vision from those on staff

2. More excellence overall
3. People will begin to see your ministry as more legitimate
4. Increased interest from non-staff members about how to join staff

C. Identify the Most Critical Roles:
Start with the most important roles, maybe even leadership roles, that you think are most critical to your current state. It is very important to get some help leading so that you don't have to be the only one handling everything that comes up.
1. Lesson from the OT:
    When we first began putting this sort of thing into place, I felt like the Lord gave me a word from the Old Testament about how the elders at the gates operated. In that culture, the city elders would gather at the city gates and when someone had an issue or a question they would go to the gate and present their case. But these elders were not all the same. The elders didn't have general authority, but they had limited jurisdiction to the particular area of their expertise. For instance an elder at the Sheep Gate had jurisdiction over matters pertaining to livestock and the economics that related to the sale of animals and related goods, but they had no authority over carpentry – that was addressed and governed elsewhere.
2. Department heads:
    We implemented our staff leadership structure according to this concept and gave people real authority over a limited area of responsibility so that the weight of their input was specific to the area that they gave leadership over. Examples in our environment included the worship department, events and finances.

D. Brainstorm Specific Job Duties:
Because each ministry looks different, you will want to sit down and think about the specifics or your environment and brainstorm what roles make sense for your context. Think about who you have on hand and how they could best help and serve your ministry. Think about what tasks and roles are absolutely necessary to the function of your prayer ministry: the prayer meetings themselves and the day-to-day operations of your ministry. Try to find ways to put people into positions that take as much of the current administrative responsibility off of your shoulders as makes sense so that you are free to invest your efforts in pioneering new areas for the ministry's growth.

Session Thirteen: From the Ground Up

I. Introduction:

I wanted to provide a single session that lays out the beginning steps 1,2 3, for those starting with nothing, because this is where most will have their start. Now that you know the why behind the what and you have been somewhat familiarized with most of the steps on how to build the house of prayer, this session is dedicated to giving a simple run down of the practical order of the first steps of how to begin. To a great degree it reviews in a concerted way several of the elements previously covered; the point is to repackage the information into a simple "how to get started" sort of presentation. For a more full review, you can look back at the sessions entitled "The Call to Build God's House," "Growth Strategies" and "A Basic Prayer Model" from which most of this session draws.

II. Things to Know Before You Begin:

A. You Will Probably Plow for Years:
It is important that you know that building the house of prayer is rigorous as well as rewarding. There is a very high probability that you will be laboring for years before things lighten up a bit. Set yourself up for the long haul and just know that you are going to want to quit many times.

B. Many Steps Don't Matter Yet:
Don't be distracted by steps that don't matter for you yet. Most of you will begin with only a handful of people; this is the majority of houses of prayer across the nation (even those based in large churches). With only a few people you don't need to worry much about many dynamics that will become important to you down the road. I've listed some things below that we are commonly approached about that fall into the "not now" category. In my opinion, almost no one is ready for the below steps

until they have been in daily prayer meetings for a season.
1. Developing the harp and bowl prayer model
2. How to do an internship
3. Financing the house of prayer
4. Developing curriculum
5. Conducting workshops and other trainings
6. Hosting a large event

C. Things Will Expand in Time:
If you are faithful with little you will be given more. Show yourself faithful to the initial building steps and don't look for shortcuts. The time of growth will come when you are ready for it, and there are plenty of additional steps you can take then.

III. Getting Started:

A. Start Daily Prayer Meetings:
1. Pick a location:
   Anywhere is fine so long as you can guarantee that you will have continued use of that space. It doesn't need to be big; an apartment living room is fine. I would far more recommend the use of your personal space than any option that doesn't guarantee you continued use (for instance a room at your church that sometimes needs to be used for another purpose).
2. Pick a time:
   As stated in previous sessions, above all else pick a time five to seven days a week that works with your schedule. Make it the same time every day at the same location so there is no confusion and people can count on where and when.
3. Plan to begin immediately:
   Do not wait. Begin immediately. Start daily prayer meetings as soon as you can, earlier than that if possible. You can always amend what you start. Most people have great intentions but put off starting, and the Devil comes and steals that desire from them. Get yourself committed to daily prayer meetings quickly.
4. Plan to personally be in all the prayer meetings:
   You need to actually be there. It's not enough that you attend some of them. If you are the leader God has called, then you need to be there for all of them in the early days.

B. Establish the Concept of Prayer Commitments:
Create a document that people can read and sign that explains what you mean by

Session 13: From the Ground Up

"commit to a prayer meeting." Spend some time developing your thoughts about this idea so that it can be clearly communicated on paper. You are welcome to take ours and amend it for your own purposes.

C. **Cast the Vision:**

Get as many people together as you have influence with (I had only a handful when we began) and cast the vision for what you're doing. Announce your start date; ask them to get involved by attending meetings and by signing up for some specific prayer shifts.

D. **Enlist Prayer Leaders:**
1. Those who seem able:
   If you've never done this, trying to pick people who will be good prayer leaders may seem a bit difficult. Right now it doesn't matter if they are good. What you are looking for when you begin is willing and able. It is likely that no one will be "good" yet.
2. Assign each to a different day:
   Give each prayer leader an assigned day, and I recommend that if possible you don't give any of them two days so as to share the load and not give opportunity for pride of one over another. You want to give yourself as much of a shot for success as possible as you launch.
3. You prayer lead at least one day:
   No matter who you are or what experience you do or do not have, it is important that you as the leader be an example before the rest of your crew. You will grow in this together, learning from each other, making mistakes together. They need to see you right there in the trenches with them.

E. **Create a Simple Prayer Model:**
1. Create daily topics:
   If you are meeting 5 times a week, then I strongly suggest having 5 different prayer focuses. Assign each day its own topic and develop subtopics under each day's theme. A poster for the wall of your living room or an overhead slide or something else visual will be very helpful to you. I have listed some theme ideas below that may help you.
   a. Thanksgiving
   b. Revival
   c. Israel
   d. Church unity

HOW TO BUILD A HOUSE OF PRAYER

      e. Evangelism

      f. The market place

2. Format your time:

    Figure out how long your prayer meetings are going to be; my suggestion is that you begin with one hour. Then format that hour up into smaller chunks of time that your prayer leaders will be in charge of facilitating. Below I have listed a very simple format for a one hour prayer meeting that may help you form your model.

    7:00-7:15 a.m. Worship (use a CD)

    7:15-7:25 a.m. Intercession (sub topic 1)

    7:25-7:30 a.m. One on one prayer for needs in the room

    7:30-7:40 a.m. Intercession (sub topic 2)

    7:40-7:50 a.m. Worship (use a CD)

    7:50-8:00 a.m. Intercession (sub topic 3)

3. Use the Bible:

    It is important that everyone is on the same page during your prayer meetings; it's the entire point of the corporate dynamic. We have found that nothing unifies us in prayer quite like the scriptures. So teach your people to begin each and every prayer by reading a scripture that has to do with the subject you are praying for. We recommend using the Apostolic Prayers in the New Testament. Below is a simple example script of what this looks like on a day when you are praying for the lost.

    a. Identify:

    "I'm going to be developing a prayer from Ephesians chapter 1 verse 17 asking the Lord to reveal Himself to the lost."

    b. Read:

    Ephesians 1:17 "I keep asking that the God of our Lord Jesus Christ, the glorious Father, may give you the Spirit of wisdom and revelation, so that you may know him better."

    c. Pray:

    "Lord, allow the lost in our city to see you, show them the falsehood of the world and the truth of who you are that they might know you."

F. Start a Weekly Gathering:

You want to begin a weekly service as soon as possible to have a rallying point where you cast vision, draw in new people and equip those who are building with you. Below I've listed some resources (a year's worth) that I would recommend you start with until you have the vision clear enough yourself to be able to teach your own messages. Each of these is multisession and will serve to lay a strong foundation for you and

Session 13: From the Ground Up

your team; make sure to have a time of discussion after each session.
1. Intro to the End Times Audio Course (The Prayer Room resource)
2. History of the Prayer Movement Course (The Prayer Room resource)
3. Tabernacle of David Study Book (The Prayer Room resource)
4. Signs of the Times Study Book (The Prayer Room resource)

G. Begin Going Deep in Personal Bible Study:
In order to sustain your own heart and have anything to give those around you, it is essential that you begin giving yourself to studying the themes that most help encourage the building of the house of prayer. I've listed what I believe to be the most important subjects below.
1. End times
2. Bridal paradigm
3. Subject of prayer
4. Sermon on the Mount

H. Invite People to Join You:
1. Pray for more laborers:
   An important prayer focus in the formative days and weeks is that God would raise up other intercessors to stand with you. It's wise to continue praying for this throughout every part of your building phase. Without God sending more intercessors, you will not be able to build beyond certain limits.
2. Active invitation:
   Team up those prayers for laborers with encouraging all involved to actively invite everyone they know. You may be surprised how many people will want to come check out a prayer meeting that meets every day.

I. Ahead of the Curve:
If you will implement all of the above steps, you will instantly be a more functional house of prayer than 90% of what is out there, at least in America. I would go as far to say that the above parameters are actually the entry point of even qualifying as a house of prayer. Most everything else probably more fits the description of an enthusiastic prayer group.

J. Persevere:
Don't give up and don't let up. It's going to take some fortitude to get started and keep things going month after month. Don't give up, press through the difficulties

and whatever you do, don't stop the prayer meetings. It will get easier but not until it gets really tough first. This tends to be the Lord's way in order to keep it precious and to refine the vessels He will use to carry the Prayer Movement.

Session Fourteen: Expanding Once You're Established

I. **Entering into the Second Phase of Your Ministry Growth:**

   A. **When It's Time:**
   There comes a time when you are sort of out of the woods, so to speak. You are no longer mostly concerned with the daily question of, "Will your ministry cease to exist because of a strong gust of wind?" You come to a point where your prayer meetings are functioning pretty well, however simple, and your ministry is established in the city to a certain degree. You find yourself in a season where it's really time to expand.

   B. **When It's Not:**
   I'll tell you painfully that it took us over three years of doing fourteen prayer meetings a week before we reached this point, so don't be disappointed if it takes you some years of fighting in the trenches before you outgrow that stage. It's been my experience that most of the houses of prayer in America haven't hit this point yet, but many are prematurely attempting to take these steps before they're ready and so the firm foundation of corporate prayer is suffering as a result.

   C. **Corporate Prayer is the Standard:**
   Corporate prayer isn't on our menu as houses of prayer, it's what we do, and we must fight to keep it that way even if it seemingly costs us looking like we're not really growing much. Truth is, most really are not growing much yet, and it's probably mostly from the Lord and not the Devil. Wait until you have firmly established your daily prayer meetings and they've been tested over a season and found able to survive some difficulty.

   D. **Starting at Phase Two:**
   Because each ministry situation is different and there are some out there who will be

enabled to begin with a stronger position than the majority, it may be advisable for some ministries to start their journey with the steps in this session. Remember that we at TPR were in the majority who certainly had to start from scratch with nothing, so don't feel bad if you have to do the same. It can be done.

E. Providing the Next Steps:

This session details some of the next steps that a growing house of prayer will probably want to implement. As with all the ideas presented in this handbook, I am going to toss out things we learned from our journey as well as insights from watching other houses of prayer. That doesn't mean this is the only way to build. Ask the Lord about the steps you are supposed to take; my hope is only to provide you with some ideas that may be helpful. There's not necessarily an order to most of these suggestions, so you'll want to prayerfully feel out what will work best in your environment.

II. Prayer Initiatives

A. Adding More Sets:

First and foremost, a growing house of prayer should be thinking about how to add more prayer meetings to the weekly schedule. To effectively create a culture of prayer, more than one daily meeting will be required. If a goal of the ministry is to eventually have lots of prayer meetings, then those have to be added one step at a time. I have listed some recommendations that we advise you to keep to as you build.

1. Add new sets across the board:

    This goes back to how you added your first prayer set, a daily time at the same time each day. Don't start adding random prayer meetings that don't fit with the schedule and pattern you have already established.

2. Pick a different time of day:

    If you pick another time of day from the time you already have going, you will be able to reach a different group of people which will help you to get more overall people involved. For instance, if you already have a 6-7am daily prayer meeting, think about how to start a 7-8pm daily meeting.

3. Hand off responsibility of the other meetings:

    Once you have your first daily prayer set established with prayer leaders and others committed to each day, then you can be free to go pioneer the next meeting. Come off all the ones that you need to and now commit to all of the new meetings just like you did when you first started. Your presence will once again be invaluable to get things started and to keep the DNA that you have fought to establish.

Session 14: Expanding Once You're Established

B. **Develop the Harp and Bowl Prayer Model:**

If you haven't already done so, at this point you want to start to figure out how to implement elements of worship and prayer together. Many of us in the prayer movement call this the Harp and Bowl model.

1. Why:

    Implementing some version of Harp and Bowl will add greatly to the enjoyment factor, and when people enjoy the prayer meetings they will keep coming.

2. How to move forward:

    We have additional resources available on how the Harp and Bowl model works when you decide that you want to figure out how it might look in your context. We could possibly send you a small team to help train your people, or you could attend a workshop at our missions base. Additionally, we also have printed resources available.

3. What:

    When we first began to implement its principles, we realized that there were many things we had to adapt and do differently from IHOP-KC (from whom we had mostly seen it modeled). The model we reformed employs all the same elements but allows for a wide range of variance in how many musicians and singers are involved. A main thing we kept running into in our early days and even today is that we don't have an overage of singers, musicians and worship leaders. We had to build our model to be able to flex for sets that only have one worship leader all the way up to sets that have a full team.

III. Develop Paid Programs:

After you've been established in your city or congregation and you believe that people might look to you as having something of value to offer, you want to start developing paid programs. We will discuss some of the administrative ways to operate internships, events, schools, etc. later in this session, but for now however, let's just focus on the finance side of things.

A. **Set-Rate Semester Long Program:**

As soon as you can begin semester long commitments, the better. We recommend starting with a three-month long internship. Programs like these have minimal cost to your ministry but can add a great deal of finances depending on how many you are able to get involved each semester. After you have figured out your approximate costs (printing, additional utility costs, other resources, etc,), then assign a set cost for your program based off the value of what you are offering.

B. Special One Time Offerings:

1. Getting new people to your base:
   This concept really only works when you can get people into the room who aren't already giving everything they have. We love to have special guest speakers come and speak at our house of prayer for a number of reasons. One reason is that these events serve to get many new faces in the door that otherwise would not have visited our missions base, and because they are there we have the opportunity to introduce them to our vision and what we are about.

2. Working out the finances:
   I will negotiate a set dollar amount honorarium with the speaker before the event so that they know we intend to compensate them for their time. Normally, as long as I set a reasonable honorarium amount, we collect more than we need, sometimes enough that we can make a little and even give more to the speaker than we promised (which is always a blessing to do when you are able).

3. Taking up the offering:
   Then on the night of the event, I'll take up an offering and ask the people to partner with us and with our guest speaker. I tell them that we have administrative costs to run our ministry and that we plan to give our guest an honorarium for being with us that night. I then invite them to help with that and tell them it would be greatly appreciated.

C. Registration Plus Offerings:

Host a conference. Figure out how much it's going to cost you and then do your best to guess at how many will attend.

1. Registration:
   Try to charge an amount that will cover all your costs but not be so expensive that people are hindered from attending.

2. Offering:
   Then at the event, take up offering each night and ask the people to partner with you and the guest speaker. Tell them that you have administrative costs to run your ministry and that you plan to give the guest an honorarium for being with you. Then tell them that it would be greatly appreciated and invite them to help.

3. Coming out ahead:
   If you gauge things rightly, you should come out considerably ahead financially on events like this. Many ministries in America survive mostly off the offerings they collect at special ministry events like conferences.

Session 14: Expanding Once You're Established

IV. Start an Internship:
A. Benefits to Your House of Prayer:
1. Casts vision for those involved
2. Gets more people into prayer meetings
3. It increases the level of involvement of those already around
4. Builds close knit community
5. Provides your ministry with finances
6. In many ways it legitimizes your ministry

B. How to Run an Internship:
1. Director:
   You will need someone to act as the internship director; most likely you need to be this person for at least the first one or two internships you conduct so you can get your hands around it and form the nuts and bolts of what you want it to look like.
2. Finances:
   Make sure to charge an appropriate amount for what you are offering the interns. If you charge nothing or too little, they won't value it and you will find them far more willing to skip classes and not fulfill other responsibilities. If you make the cost too high, however, then no one will sign up; it's more than they can't afford it –it actually has to do with assessing value. If they don't think your program is worth $500, then they aren't going to pay $500. Maybe start off with something more like $100 for your first run at it.
3. Curriculum:
   You can always supplement internship curriculum by using resources from other ministries like The Prayer Room or others you know of. We do highly recommend, however, that you begin to draft at least some of your own teaching resources from the very start. The long-term growth and success of your paid programs will require you to develop your own teaching resources, so now is the best time to start because to accumulate even a few teaching courses of your own will take you a while.
4. Content and purpose:
   You want to have some goals in mind for what you hope the interns will take away from their time in your internship. You want them to come out of it with a greater vision for why to give themselves to night and day prayer, with a servant attitude and better equipped to lead prayer meetings at your house of prayer. Form your program around these things so that you are graduating those who can help fuel your house.

HOW TO BUILD A HOUSE OF PRAYER

C. Elements of an Internship:
1. Prayer meeting commitments
2. Weekly classes (possibly multiple times a week)
3. Service shift of some sort
4. Attendance at your weekly service

D. Promoting Your Internship:
1. Where to promote:
   a. At your weekly meeting
   b. Heavily through email
   c. One on one conversations
   d. Any small groups you can present to
2. Selling points:
   a. A season of consecration
   b. A way to build community
   c. A time of vision casting
   d. A great way to slow down
   e. Lots of time in the Word
   f. Lots of hours per week in prayer
3. Promotional resources:
   a. Develop an internship pamphlet
   b. Put up to date info on your website
   c. Create and hang up posters about it

V. Next Step for Your Events:

A. Conducting Monthly Workshops:
Free monthly workshops are fairly easy to pull off and provide a great on ramp to continually get new people in the door.
1. What is required?:
   The great thing is that beyond promotion all you need to pull off a two-hour workshop is a place and a person. Ask someone in your community who has an area of strength to spend some weeks preparing and then have them teach and lead the workshop for you.
2. Topic ideas:
   a. The Harp and Bowl model

Session 14: Expanding Once You're Established

       b. Marketplace Christianity
       c. Growing in the prophetic
       d. Cultivating a prayer life
       e. Healing and deliverance
       f. Equipping children
       g. God's heart for Israel

B. Begin One-Day Seminars:
One day seminars can be a great entry into conference ministry without all the risk. Plan an all day Saturday event that includes registration and a variety of sessions. Advertise your one-day seminar using your own worship leaders and teachers. By using in house teachers you will save money and this will also help you begin to develop your own curriculum. Below are some suggested one-day seminar topics.
1. Ministry of the Holy Spirit
2. Intro to the end times
3. Prayer and missions
4. Vision and values of the house of prayer

C. Host a Larger Event:
When you're ready to hold your first conference, we suggest that you bring in a speaker from someplace else (probably in the prayer movement). People may not come from all over to hear you speak on an issue, but by bringing someone in you can draw people by use of the speaker's specific set of expertise or his or her name recognition; use these to promote and draw people to your event. If you want to do a conference on the end times, then find a teacher who has some real revelation on that subject and invite them. If you are wanting to really focus on worship at your conference maybe you should bring in a well known worship leader instead of a speaker. If you plan and promote it well within your sphere of influence, then you should be able to draw many new faces and come out ahead on the finances.

VI. Getting into a Larger Space:
You may not be ready for 24/7 prayer yet, but if you are growing in numbers and you are adding prayer sets its probably time to start thinking about your own space or a larger place depending on what you began with. This section only applies to ministries that are outgrowing their current space and are in need of either more square footage to accomplish everything you want to do or that you are running into schedule conflicts that are

preventing you from doing what you want.

A. Common Growth Needs:
1. Your space is now too small for your weekly service
2. You cannot realistically add more prayer sets in your current setup
3. You have no place to hold additional trainings or internships
4. You now have need of something nicer or more permanent

B. Use of Space:
Up to this point you have probably been using someone's space; perhaps an office break room or someone's living room or maybe a room at your church. You may decide that has been working fine and that you want to continue with some version of that plan with just a larger space allocated or more times at the same location. If you continue to grow then it is likely that you will eventually need something to change, but if additional space is available for you and things are working, then great. One great thing about this option is that it's relatively cheap or even free which allows you to invest your resources on other aspects of the ministry.

C. Leasing:
Once you decide to leave the comfort of free space, your options start to get expensive. You will end up with greatly increased monthly expenses. You can lease some space or attempt to purchase something. We will begin with leasing. There are both benefits and drawbacks to leasing.

1. Benefits:
   Many times you can get into a lease with little credit and nothing down, except maybe a month's rent as a security deposit. You're not locked into that location long term, so if you have reason to relocate you can probably do so fairly easily at the end of your lease.
2. Drawbacks:
   Whatever finances you pour into that place are going to be lost when you leave there, and there is no guarantee that you will be there long term. You will have the responsibility of navigating your landlord, who may or may not like your loud music all the time. We had to build a $3500 sound proof wall in our lease space because the neighbors kept complaining even after we had turned the music down to a much lower and manageable level.

D. Owning:
Your other option is to try to figure out how you might be able to purchase a building

for your ministry which is probably the most ideal situation, but I have listed both the positives and negatives on this avenue as well.

1. Benefits:

    If you are able to pull it off, owning your own space is ideal because you can do with the space whatever you want. You don't have a landlord who can put you out of business, and you can always remodel or add to your facility.

2. Drawbacks:

    It is very difficult for a small ministry to get a large enough loan to make such a purchase. If you are able to get a loan, it will doubtlessly require that you come up with tens of thousands of dollars (or more) as a down payment. Owning a building will lock you in long-term, so make sure that you are where you want to be.

VII. Building an Equipping Center:

The concept of an equipping center is quite a different reality from simply running an internship program (though it would probably include an internship). The way I'm defining an equipping center is a multi-program based school, almost a university on a small scale. The purpose of such a place is to provide in depth training on multiple different subjects and equip people for a variety of assignments. The strength of offering multiple focuses is that you will be able to appeal to a larger audience.

A. Organization:

You will employ many of the same strategies that you are already using in running your internship but with a greater focus, higher level of excellence and more organization.

1. Add one program or school at a time (start with your internship)
2. At this point you will need to develop your own curriculum
3. Develop your programs into semesters (run in line with local colleges)
4. Programs probably should remain part time in commitment

B. Strengthening Your Internship:

To start with, you will want to revamp your internship to make it as appealing of an offering as possible. Focus on several key aspects.

1. Curriculum:
    a. If it's not interesting, no one will want to do it
    b. If it's not your own material, they'll just go to the source to study it
    c. If it's not well written, they will give it poor reviews afterward
    d. Teachers must be clear in the presentation or you'll get poor reviews

2. Promotional materials:
   Now is the time to step up your branding and graphic design. We live in a generation that is used to seeing well done promotional materials, and you will actually lose a large percentage of your target audience if you don't make your program visually appealing.
3. Staple elements:
   a. Weekly prayer meetings
   b. Attendance at your weekly service
   c. Some sort of service shift
   d. Daily internship classes
   e. Participation on a fasting team
4. Value adders:
   Because part of the plan is to increase the program cost, you will want to revamp your internship to include some value adders. This can vary greatly, but I have listed some ideas below that are fairly easy upgrades.
   a. A fun graduation party
   b. An hour one on one with a member of your leadership team
   c. Printed curriculum books
   d. Additional required reading (provide the books)
   e. Additional required listening (provide the MP3s)
   f. Free participation in a conference that semester

C. **Elements of a Music Academy:**
   A separate school of music will create a unique appeal to musicians and singers. While you will probably utilize most all of the principles listed for the internship, you want to repackage them slightly so that each program has a distinct feel and isn't just a photocopy of the other schools you offer.
   1. Curriculum:
      a. Include elements of music theory
      b. Include elements of team ministry
      c. Include elements of theology of worship
      d. Bring in speakers who can really add to your program
   2. Staple elements:
      a. Weekly prayer meetings
      b. Attendance at your weekly service
      c. Weekly music academy specific classes
      d. Participation on multiple worship teams
      e. Weekly practice on their instrument or in song writing

Session 14: Expanding Once You're Established

D. Elements of a Bible School:

There may be better ways to go about it, but the process we used at TPR which worked great was to establish our internship first, then our Forerunner Music Academy and then to work on launching our part time Bible School. We spent some years building up our curriculum before we were able to really launch our FSM (Forerunner School of Ministry). Curriculum is the key. You need at least 5 of your own courses (12-16 sessions each) before you can even launch your first semester.

1. Our structure:

   We decided that we would run our internship and FSM in dynamic overlap, wherein our interns participate in whatever classes are being offered that semester at the Bible School as their internship curriculum. This has served us well because it introduces our interns to the Bible School, and if they want to continue to take classes after their internship, they can. Our interns take these FSM classes at no additional charge – their tuition is included in their internship cost.

2. Individual class requirements:

   Students can commit to attend as little as one class per week if they like and as many as all of the classes offered that semester. All FSM classes require that students choose one prayer meeting per course they are attending. Prayer meeting attendance is not optional; it is part of the course requirement, as we are offering a unique form of education which is bathed in night and day prayer.

3. Costs:

   We recommend charging somewhere around $75 or more per class when offered individually. You may decide to give a break on the cost when someone signs up for the entire semester.

E. Other Training Programs:

Depending on your unique mandates and strengths, you may decide to offer additional training programs that meet another need within your region or community. Offer as many programs as makes sense and as you can operate well. Scale back if you find that attendance is too low to justify keeping them all. Some suggestions.

1. Keep your internship running every semester (including summer)
2. Rotate the rest of your programs, not offering all of them all the time
3. Keep each program distinct from each other
4. Always be looking for ways to improve / add value to your programs

ABOUT THE AUTHOR

Brad Stroup and his wife Amy reside in Dallas area with their three children where he serves as director of The Prayer Room Missions Base. This is a developing 24/7 house of prayer with live worship 22 hours a day run by a few full and part time staff members and a small army of volunteers. They have been holding daily corporate prayer meetings 7 days a week since September 13, 2005 and grown the ministry into a flourishing city-wide prayer reality with people coming from over 100 churches. Brad is a student of the Word of God and has been an enthusiastic Bible teacher for over 20 years now. For the past 10 years he's felt commissioned by the Lord to give specific focus to end times related themes. He spent three years teaching through the Book of Revelation theme by theme, committed a three-year period of time where he prayrfully read through the Book of Revelation every week and has been teaching end time subjects near weekly for the last decade. Out of the overflow of this teaching ministry Brad started the Forerunner Equipping Center; a part time training school that focuses on equipping this generation to love the Lord with all their heart and make ready for His return. Brad also leads a national network of houses of prayer and travels around the US offering consulting to churches, HOPs and ministries wanting to cultivate a culture of prayer. Over the years Brad has been able to encourage dozens of houses of prayer, helping many to get started and strengthening others at various stages in their journey.

Would you like to invite Brad or another one of The Prayer Room's teachers to speak at your church, organization or event? If so, please contact us at info@tprdfw.com to schedule a speaker and arrange details.

PRESENCE PIONEERS MEDIA

Check out these other titles by Presence Pioneers Media

10 DAYS
by Jonathan Friz

ENJOYING PRAYER
by Matthew Lilley

DAVID'S TABERNACLE
by Matthew Lilley

Available wherever you buy books or at
presencepioneers.org

To get updates and discounts on future book releases visit media.presencepioneers.org or scan the QR code below